PRAISE FOR
Creative Visualization for Writers

"Nina Amir delivers an inspiring book that offers solutions to the problems creative people struggle with: *What is my vision, and how can I access it and make it come true in the real world?* Every creative work in the world starts with an idea and the problem of how to bring it forth. *Creative Visualization for Writers* draws upon ancient wisdom and modern techniques to help you give birth to your project."

—LINDA JOY MYERS, PRESIDENT OF THE NATIONAL ASSOCIATION OF MEMOIR WRITERS AND AUTHOR OF *THE POWER OF MEMOIR* AND GOLD MEDAL WINNER *DON'T CALL ME MOTHER*

. . . .

"*Creative Visualization for Writers* is brilliant—a guidebook, journal, writing coach, coloring book, and touchpoint to your inner life, all in one place! I love the blend of introspection and activity, along with the short, actionable chapters and exercises. Nina Amir's holistic approach can help you be creative, productive, and successful as a writer—and enjoy a rompin' good time in the process. This book will help you choose the right projects—the ones that truly light your fire and help you live your purpose now—and complete them."

—LISA TENER, AUTHOR AND BOOK COACH (WWW.LISATENER.COM)

. . . .

"In *Creative Visualization for Writers*, Nina Amir shares all you need to know to implement the latest research on how your brain tap into its very own writing genius."

—CAROLYN HOWARD-JOHNSON, MULTI-AWARD-WINNING POET AND AUTHOR OF THE HOWTODOITFRUGALLY SERIES OF BOOKS FOR WRITERS

"More than just a map, *Creative Visualization for Writers* is like a GPS for achieving your writing dreams. I highlighted the heck out of this book!"

—CARLA KING, MISADVENTURES MEDIA

. . . .

"An inspiring guide to help you get to know your inner writer—and decode how to truly work alongside her to produce your best writing."

—ZACHARY PETIT, EDITOR, *PRINT* MAGAZINE

. . . .

""With powerful, affirming messages of support, Creative Visualization will help any writer harness the positive energy and creativity necessary to do their best work. Nina Amir's confident, encouraging voice will motivate writers on their discouraged days, and inspire in the best of times."

—JORDAN ROSENFELD, AUTHOR OF *WRITING THE INTIMATE CHARACTER*,
A *WRITER'S GUIDE TO PERSISTENCE* AND FIVE OTHER BOOKS

. . . .

"This delightful, interactive book brings to writers the awesome power of visualization and combines it with Nina Amir's wise, sane advice on how to get your work out of your head and into the world. It's a must-read for aspiring authors who want to become published."

—JOEL FRIEDLANDER (WWW.THEBOOKDESIGNER.COM)

. . . .

"I love the concept of this book. The writing process is never straightforward. Right-brain exercises, from visualizing to coloring, can add joy to rote tasks like outlining and marketing. At the same time, goal-setting and list-making activities can spark creative thinking. So let your creativity and productivity flow together!"

—JODY REIN, LITERARY AGENT AND CO-AUTHOR OF
HOW TO WRITE A BOOK PROPOSAL FIFTH EDITION

Creative
VISUALIZATION
FOR
Writers

Nina Amir

WRITER'S DIGEST
BOOKS

WritersDigest.com
Cincinnati, Ohio

For more resources for writers, visit www.writersdigest.com.

20 19 18 17 16 5 4 3 2 1

Distributed in Canada by Fraser Direct
100 Armstrong Avenue
Georgetown, Ontario, Canada L7G 5S4
Tel: (905) 877-4411

Distributed in the U.K. and Europe by F&W Media International
Brunel House, Newton Abbot, Devon, TQ12 4PU, England
Tel: (+44) 1626-323200, Fax: (+44) 1626-323319
E-mail: postmaster@davidandcharles.co.uk

ISBN-13: 978-1-4403-4718-4

Edited by Rachel Randall
Designed by Alexis Estoye
Illustrations by Zach Nicholas
Production coordinated by Debbie Thomas

Dedication

To all those who want to turn their vision of becoming a writer or author into a reality. And to the people in my life who help me keep my visions alive and make them real.

ACKNOWLEDGMENTS

I would like to thank the following people:

My literary agent, Gordon Warnock, who provides me with phenomenal guidance, pushes me to be my best, helps me succeed, and is my publishing partner in the truest sense.

Phil Sexton, who takes a chance on my ideas and turns them into books that help bring more aspiring authors' books into the world.

Rachel Randall, for making my manuscripts shine and asking me to stretch as a writer.

The team at Writer's Digest Books, for producing phenomenal books, including mine: Alexis Estoye, Debbie Thomas, Lynn DeRocco, and Michael Hanna.

All the teachers, including Shakti Gawain, from whom I learned that thoughts are creative and the mind's power to visualize helps you intentionally bring your ideas and desires to life. Your wisdom has helped me make a positive and meaningful difference in the world.

My friends and family members (you know who you are), who remind me consciously and deliberately to create my ideas, career, and life.

My husband and children, who support my work and listen to me babble on incessantly about how they, too, can manifest the life and career of their dreams.

About the Author

Nina Amir is an Amazon best-selling author of such books as *How to Blog a Book* and *The Author Training Manual*. She is known as the Inspiration-to-Creation Coach because she helps writers and other creative people combine their passion and purpose so they move from idea to inspired action and **A**chieve **M**ore **I**nspired **R**esults. This helps them positively and meaningfully impact the world—with their words or other creations.

Nina is a hybrid author who has self-published seventeen books and had as many as nine books on Amazon's Top 100 lists and six on the same bestseller list (Authorship) at the same time.

As an Author Coach, Nina supports writers on the journey to successful authorship. Some of her clients have sold 300,000+ copies of their books, landed deals with major publishing houses, and created thriving businesses around their books. She is the creator of a proprietary Author Training curriculum for writers and coaches.

She is an international speaker, award-winning journalist, and multi-site blogger as well as the founder of National Nonfiction Writing Month and the Nonfiction Writers' University.

Nina also is one of three hundred elite Certified High Performance Coaches working around the world.

Table of Contents

SELF-EXPLORATION

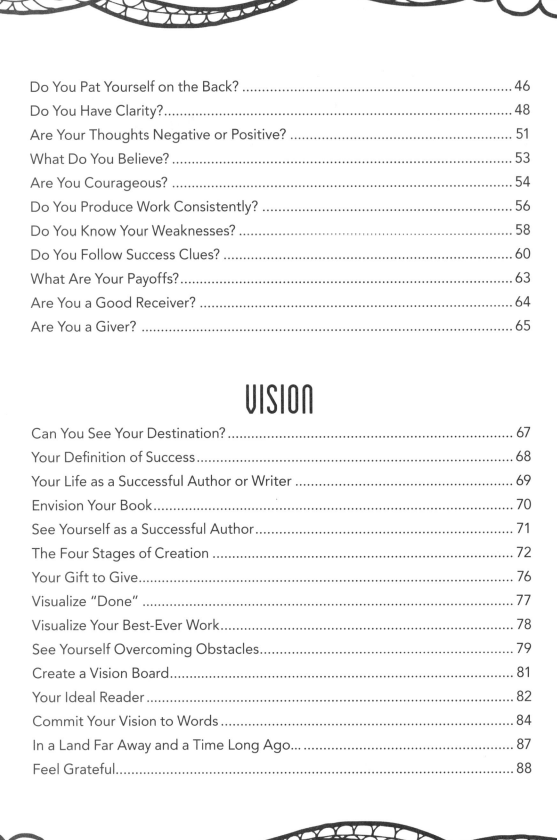

VISION

GOALS

CREATIVITY

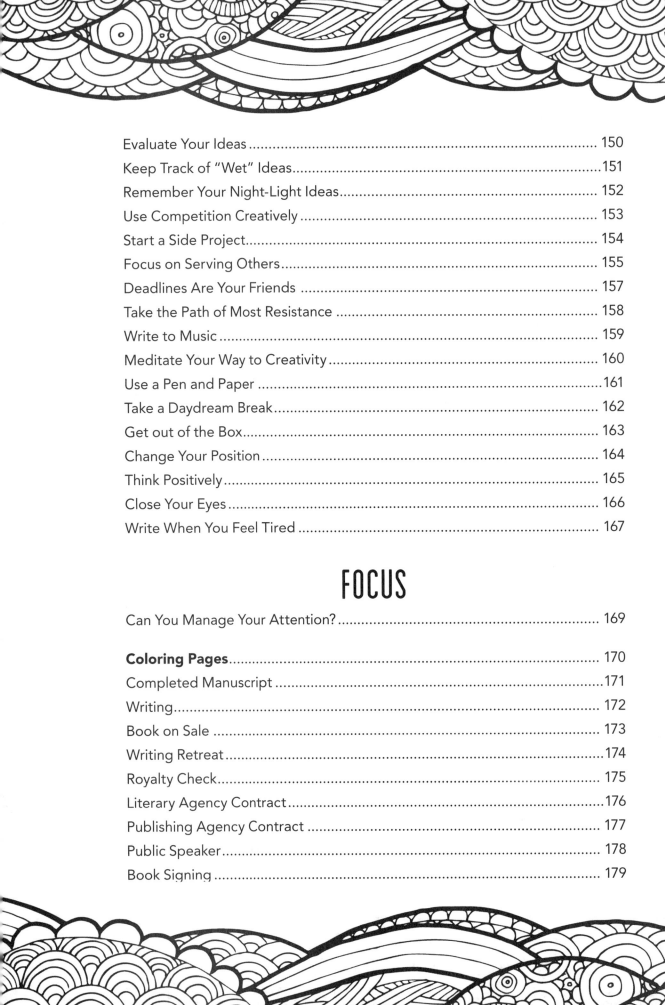

FOCUS

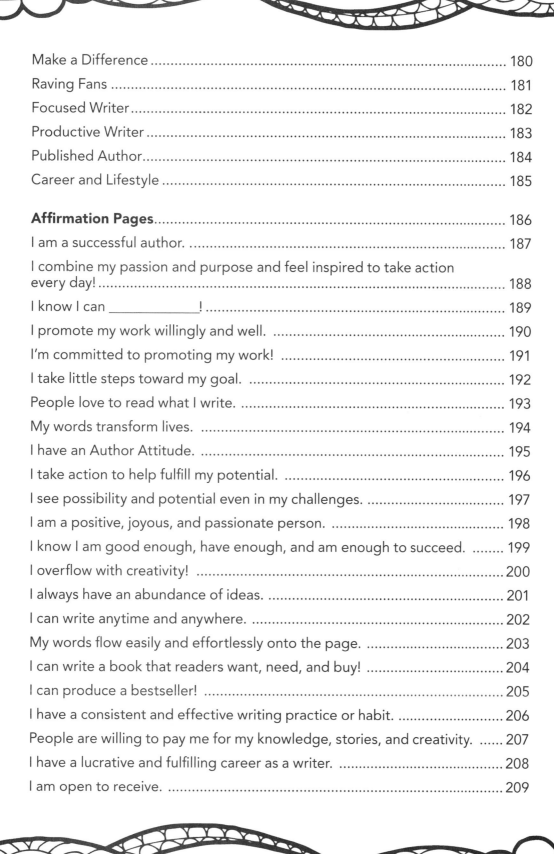

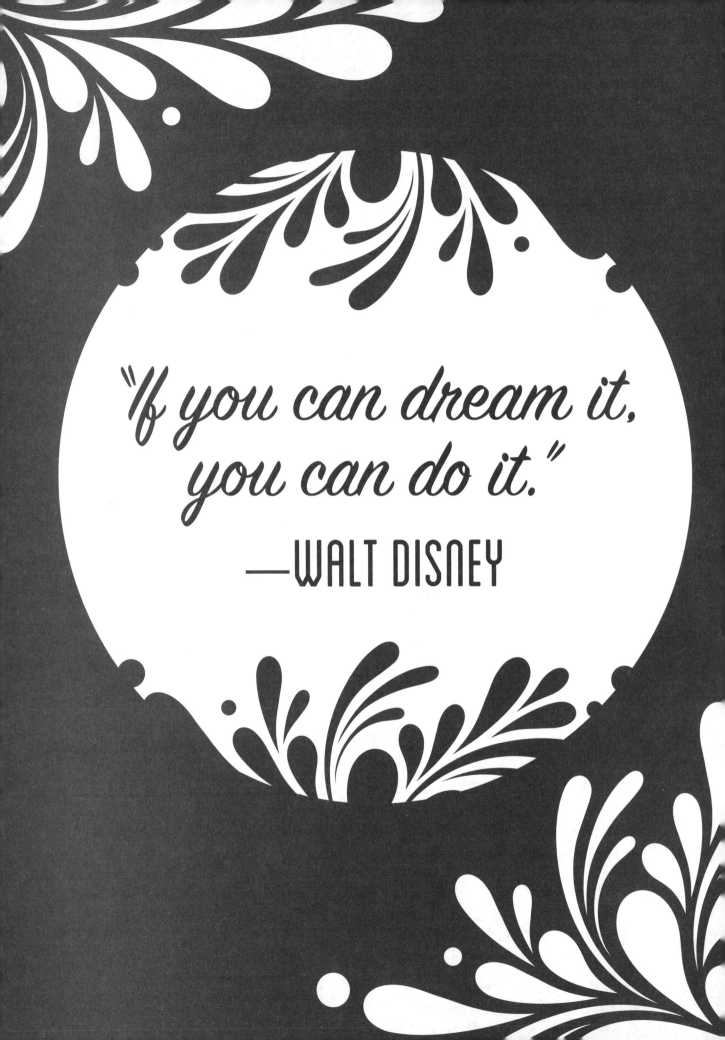

"If you can dream it, you can do it."

—WALT DISNEY

Foreword

My journey into the creative process began behind the lens of a camera, first with still photography and then with shooting and editing rough footage for independent documentary films. From there I moved to the acting studio and then to modern dance classes. Eventually I traveled with an experimental theater troupe, touring the eastern seaboard in a beat-up old van, but, in my roundabout way, that experience ultimately convinced me that what I really wanted to do was become a writer.

At the time—young, lacking much confidence, feeling the need to somehow "establish" myself as an artist—all of this hopping around felt like failure, an innate inability to focus my efforts.

Only later did I come to see that my circuitous path had, in fact, been quite useful. Along the way, each of these art forms—visual storytelling, acting, dance—taught me lessons about creativity that have served me well throughout my literary career.

While writing, in its simplest definition, is the act of stringing together words into some arrangement that provides recognizable meaning, creative writing calls on parts of the brain far removed from our language-processing centers. What I learned from my forays into the visual and performative arts is that creativity in all forms demands intuition, imagination, openness to the unexpected, and—yes—daydreaming. Sometimes stepping out your front door and staring for a moment into the cloud-speckled sky can be a productive use of an artist's time. Perhaps that's why some people find us odd.

While these lessons took nearly a decade of my life to learn, Nina Amir's interactive workbook, *Creative Visualization for Writers*, would have saved me some time.

Drawing on the work of Shakti Gawain, Amir begins by examining the inner artist—our motivations, our aspirations, our doubts and obstacles—and then offers a pleasingly wide array of methods for artists to harness the mental and creative energy needed to produce stories, poems, essays, memoirs, or whatever work lies ahead.

Rather than reiterating the (certainly useful but available elsewhere) nuts and bolts of quality writing—active nouns and verbs, musicality of language, clear imagery and metaphor, sensory detail—this workbook focuses on the other challenges all artists face: vision, intentionality, goal-setting, persistence, clarity. Many of the exercises she offers provide easy, effective methods to move beyond the voices and uncertainties often labeled "writer's block."

Just as athletes need to stretch their muscles each morning before setting off on the track or mounting the bike, we writers, Amir reminds us, need to stretch our brains. "You may need to get out of your mind," she writes. "Or you might need to stretch it or set it on more useful thoughts. At the least, you need to learn how to use your mind in different ways and to its full capacity."

Many of us don't use our minds to full capacity, and that's a shame because we've been gifted with an intellect full of boundless surprise and mystery.

Speaking of surprise, *Creative Visualization for Writers* includes result-focused coloring book pages and an invitation to pull out our crayons and colored pencils.

Perhaps it is time I learn another art form. Perhaps it is time we all do.

—Dinty W. Moore

DINTY W. MOORE is the author of numerous books, including *Dear Mister Essay Writer Guy, Crafting the Personal Essay, The Accidental Buddhist*, and more. He has been published in *The Southern Review, The Georgia Review, Harpers, The New York Times Sunday Magazine*, and *Gettysburg Review*, among numerous other venues. Dinty lives in Athens, Ohio, where he grows heirloom tomatoes and edible dandelions and teaches a crop of brilliant undergraduate and graduate students as director of Ohio University's creative writing program.

Become a Visionary

"Imagination is everything. It's the preview of life's coming attractions." —**ALBERT EINSTEIN**

Visualize what you want to create. In your mind's eye, see your ideas brought to life. Imagine yourself as a successful writer, author, and authorpreneur. Your mental images and ability to use your mind spark your passion and inspire you to take actions that help you achieve your goals and realize your dreams.

I first heard the term *creative visualization* from Shakti Gawain, author of the best-selling guide that bears the same name. Before that, I studied creative thought, also called conscious or deliberate creation, a principle based on the idea that your thoughts have a creative energy—the ability to manifest your desires in the physical world. If you focus your thoughts on what you want to create, you develop the ability to bring those things into physical reality.

Gawain's book describes how to harness that mental and creative energy. She writes, "Creative visualization is the technique of using your imagination to create what you want in your life. … It's your natural power of imagination, the basic creative energy of the universe, which you constantly use, whether or not you are aware of it."

According to Gawain, "Imagination is the ability to create an idea, a mental picture, or a feeling sense of something. In creative visualization, you use your imagination to create a clear image, idea, or feeling of something you wish to manifest. Then you continue to focus on the idea, feeling, or picture regularly, giving it positive energy until it becomes objective reality … in other words, until you actually achieve what you have been imagining."

Gawain wasn't the first or only one to teach this principle. Playwright George Bernard Shaw said, "Imagination is the beginning of creation. You imagine what you desire, you will what you imagine, and, at last, you create what you will." And inspirational writer William Arthur Ward shared, "If you can imagine it, you can achieve it. If you can dream it, you can become it."

Sounds simple, right? Frequently imagine what you desire, and bring it to life. Use the power of your creative and mental energy to focus on a vision of your future and make it a reality. Become a visionary and, at the same time, a creator.

Indeed, the process is simple and effective but not always easy. Our minds tend to wander—often to what we *don't* want to create rather than to what we *do* want to create.

That's where this interactive guide comes in.

You might spend a lot of time daydreaming about becoming an author or developing a successful writing career. Your mind frequently plays with ideas for books, articles, essays, and blog posts, and you imagine what it would be like to achieve your goals and your potential. Awesome!

Here's the thing: These activities help, but consciously envisioning your goals—*deliberately daydreaming*—does much more to actualize your ideas, goals, and dreams than letting your mind wander aimlessly. It also trains your mind to focus on what you want instead of dwelling on what you don't.

Creative Visualization for Writers shows you how to daydream deliberately and consciously—to creatively visualize. The process sparks your desire to act upon your ideas, move toward your writing goals, and create a career as a successful writer and author.

This book also teaches you how to focus the power of your mind on the thoughts and beliefs that help—rather than hinder—your progress. As someone who continually works with words and thoughts, you may get stuck in your head. Your mind can become a roadblock on your journey to complete your projects and achieve your goals and dreams.

You may need to get out of your mind. Or you might need to stretch it or set it on more useful thoughts. At the least, you need to learn how to use your mind in different ways and to its full capacity. The exercises included in this creative journal help you do just that. They show you how to use both sides of your brain, all your creative and imaginative talents, and the proven tools of visualization and affirmation to make your writing ideas and career real. They support your authentic expression as a creator and an ideator so you tap into your creativity and fulfill your potential and purpose as a writer.

Of course, you must still act on your vision. The creative exercises in this book will inspire and direct you to do so.

It's time to create your future as a writer—to bring your ideas and vision of success to life.

Create Your Ideas

"Dream lofty dreams, and as you dream, so you shall become. Your vision is the promise of what you shall one day be; your ideal is the prophecy of what you shall at last unveil." —JAMES ALLEN

Writers write—but sometimes they don't.

You dream of becoming a successful writer or author and creating a livelihood from your written projects. Yet how many of your ideas remain trapped in your head? How many projects have you started but never finished?

If you want to become a writer—and a successful one—don't wait (or procrastinate) any longer. Retrieve your ideas and projects from wherever you've stowed them: your filing cabinet, computer folders, or mind. Turn them into published essays, articles, blog posts, and books. To become a writer, you must write … and publish.

With the help of this book, you can harness your mental, emotional, and physical energy to go from idea to action and from action to publication as you also develop the writing career you desire.

Why Do You Write?

Some people write because they feel compelled to do so. They *must* write.

Other writers write to be read. They want their work to affect readers in positive and meaningful ways, or they want to share a story or a message.

Some people like to say they are writers, but they only daydream about their writing ideas and goals. They don't write or put their ideas into action.

Then there are those who wait for the proverbial light bulb to blink on before beginning to write. Even after an idea comes, sometimes they reject it and end up believing they have no worthy ideas at all.

No matter why you write or the type of writer you are, you can develop the ability to illuminate and create ideas. When the light bulb turns on, you can generate the energy to take mental, emotional, and physical action on your idea.

Indeed, it takes follow-through to bring an idea into the world. If you don't do something, you'll find it difficult—nay, impossible—to create the writing career you desire.

The Power of Using Both Sides of Your Brain

Ideas begin in your mind. The ability to breathe life into those ideas relies on how you respond to what happens in your brain. For this reason, you need to learn to harness all the talents your mind possesses.

Your brain has two hemispheres, and each serves your creative endeavors differently. The right side of the brain focuses on visual stimuli. It processes information in an intuitive and simultaneous way, seeing the entire picture first and then the details. The left brain focuses on verbal stimuli. It processes information analytically and sequentially, first seeing the pieces and then combining them to produce the whole. You naturally use one side of the brain more than the other, but the two sides of your brain work together.

Left Brain

Logic
Analysis
Sequencing
Linear
Mathematics
Language
Facts
Think in Words
Computation

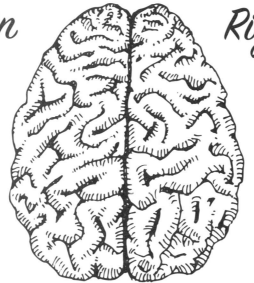

Right Brain

Creativity
Imagination
Holistic Thinking
Intuition
Arts
Rhythm
Daydreaming
Feelings
Visualization

If you write fiction, you might rely on your right brain—the creative center—more often to craft realistic characters, vibrant settings, and engaging dialogue. If you write nonfiction, on the other hand, you might use your left brain—the language center—more often as you analyze data, research topics, and present your arguments and ideas clearly and concisely.

You can strengthen the less dominant side of your brain and benefit from those newfound capacities. However, creativity studies in neuroscience suggest that the right-brain/left-brain distinction offers an incomplete picture of how the mind implements creativity. In fact, it's possible that creativity and your ability to create do not involve one side of the brain to the exclusion of the other.

Numerous interacting conscious and unconscious cognitive processes, as well as emotions, get involved when you have an idea for an article, essay, blog post, or book and begin to write. Depending on where you are in the creative process and what you want to create, you might need to call on different regions of the brain for assistance.

Thus, you'll experience heightened states of creativity and an increased ability to create when you actively engage both sides of the brain—when you write, draw, visualize, feel, and analyze. A more whole-brain approach to your work helps you generate—and realize—ideas.

That's why this book offers you opportunities to use all of your brain. It asks you to color, draw, write affirmations and visions, develop goals, visualize, journal, and evaluate your ideas.

The Power of Employing Your Artistic Ability

These pages ask you to become a multifaceted artist. You will draw and color as well as write. In the process, ideating, writing, and realizing your dreams and goals become easier.

Today, writers must do so much more than write. They must worry about submitting, publishing, and promoting their work; building an author platform and brand; and meeting deadlines. This may cause you to feel overwhelmed or stressed from time to time. Or you might experience anxiety or fear about sharing your writing (and yourself) with the world. You may feel uncomfortable digging into old emotional wounds but know it's necessary to produce your best work.

Coloring and drawing soothe these ills. Adult coloring books and art therapy are popular outlets for those in need of relaxation, focus, and healing. Art therapy helps people express feelings too difficult to put into words. Coloring also reduces symptoms of physical and emotional distress and allows you to be present in the moment, which is necessary if you get stressed and distracted by information and task overload.

Keep in mind that you don't have to be Picasso to ignite your creativity through drawing, just as you don't have to be a child to reap the benefits of coloring. No matter your artistic ability, these activities help you manage your attention, quiet your mind, and allow ideas to germinate.

The Power of Color

As you use this interactive guide, consider the hues you use to color, draw, and write. Your color choices influence your results.

Chromotherapy, or color therapy, dates back thousands of years to ancient Egypt, China, and India. Its adherents believe each color has its own wavelength and energy. Color consists of light energy and, therefore, affects us on physical, spiritual, and emotional levels.

In the business and artistic world, branding experts, marketers, and graphic artists implement the "psychology of colors" in advertisements, product packaging, and more. This principle helps them deliberately choose colors to elicit particular emotions, moods, feelings, and actions.

You can do the same by choosing specific-colored writing utensils and drawing and coloring with the hues you believe will enhance your experience and results as you work through the exercises in this book. For example, you might use red if you want to feel confident, courageous, or loving. Or you could use orange for endurance, cheerfulness, or enthusiasm. Purple gives you a sense of power, royalty, or spirituality. (You can find many websites that explain the meaning and energy of colors, should chromotherapy interest you.)

The Power of Thoughts and Beliefs

Here's another reason to add coloring to your writer's toolbox: Concentrating on coloring an image may facilitate the replacement of negative thoughts and images with more positive ones, according to Dr. Joel Pearson, a brain scientist at the University of New South Wales in Australia. Limiting beliefs and negative thoughts stop you from writing or pursuing worthwhile ideas. Since your thoughts and beliefs affect your actions, ridding yourself of unsupportive ones makes a huge difference in your ability to produce and share written work and create a successful writing career.

Third-wave psychologists stress the need to modify how you perceive thoughts so they don't control your behavior. They encourage mindfulness, the meditation-inspired practice of observing thoughts without getting entangled in them. Their advice: Acknowledge your negative thoughts, and let them go.

If mindfulness isn't your thing, follow the advice of neurolinguistics practitioners. They suggest accepting that you have negative beliefs, thoughts, and problems and then focusing your attention on what you value or want to create. For example, don't tell yourself not to think about the possibility of your book getting rejected. Trying to force yourself not to think about something rarely works. Instead, acknowledge the thought, let it go, and then say an affirmation, such as, "I share my work, and it gets published, which allows me to share my story, help people, and make a positive difference in the world."

Affirmations provide a staple strategy in personal-development circles for transforming negative thoughts and beliefs into positive ones. These positive, often future-tense statements about what you want to create or who you want to become replace negative thoughts and limiting beliefs that prevent you from creating what you desire. For example, you might affirm, "I am a published author," "I write easily and effortlessly every day," or "I courageously continue writing, no matter what."

Affirmations focus your thoughts on what you desire. However, they must be accompanied by personal-development work, especially if you suffer from low self-esteem. When coupled with a personal-development program, they prove quite powerful.

The Power of Personal Development

Personal development involves self-evaluation; consciously changing thoughts, beliefs, and habits; and deliberately choosing your actions and way of being in the world, among other methods for growth and positive change. Successful people in every industry invest in personal development, and you can use the same tools and strategies. The legendary entrepreneur and motivational speaker Jim Rohn said, "Your level of success will rarely exceed your level of personal development."

American industrialist Henry Ford said, "If you keep on doing what you've always done, you'll keep on getting what you've always got." Many successful writers use personal-development tools to level up by finding ways to think, believe, and behave differently. They use personal-development strategies to help them take bold and inspired action on their ideas and fulfill their personal and professional potential and purpose.

Like them, you need a successful attitude to bring your ideas and career to fruition. Thoughts and be-

liefs determine your attitude or mind-set. Self-talk and self-perception affect your ability to bring ideas into the world and take action toward your goals. How you feel as you move toward those goals makes a difference in your ability to achieve them.

Studies show that those who have an optimistic attitude deal with stress more effectively and achieve success more often. They aren't put off by challenges. Instead, they see them as opportunities to grow and improve.

According to author and personal-development expert Brian Tracy, "As an individual, you become what you think about most of the time. You become the sum-total result of the ideas, information, and impressions you feed into your mind, from the time you get up in the morning until you go to bed at night."

Your positive and negative habits form based on your internal landscape. Tracy claims that 95 percent of everything you do or say is determined by your habits. "Successful people have good habits that lead them to engage in positive, productive behaviors and improve their personal development throughout their lives," he says. "Unsuccessful people have inadvertently developed bad habits that cause them to act, or fail to act, in ways that lead to underachievement and failure."

The Power of Consciousness, Attention, and Intention

When you combine your thoughts and feelings, you attract what you desire. Many anecdotal stories support this theory, known as the Law of Attraction, or conscious or deliberate creation.

As author James Allen said, "You are today where your thoughts have brought you; you will be tomorrow where your thoughts take you." The Law of Attraction broke out of the New Age movement and entered the mainstream with the release of the

...d movie *The Secret*. However, long before that, Napoleon Hill talked about how to *Think and Grow Rich* in his bestseller. The late Dr. Wayne Dyer and Deepak Chopra, along with Shakti Gawain and a slew of other well-known authors, have shared their own take on the idea that you can create by focusing your thoughts on what you desire and charging them with your feelings of having already manifested it.

Remain open to the fact that thoughts, feelings, beliefs, and attitudes affect your experiences and your ability to create what you desire—a successful writing career. For example, if you wake up in the morning with the belief that today might be the day you get an acceptance letter from a literary agent, you'll feel and behave differently than if you woke up convinced that no one will ever offer you a contract for your book. In the first case, you would feel and act positive, hopeful, happy, and energetic, and behave in ways that align with your dream. In the second, you would feel negative, hopeless, unhappy, and lethargic, and probably do little or nothing to further your goal.

Will you attract an agent with positivity alone? Maybe. To a great extent, your book idea, query, platform, and writing skill determine this, but your positive attitude will keep you focused on what you need to do and how to do it, and your self-confidence will be contagious. Conversely, a negative attitude might push away a potential agent. It comes across energetically in all you do and will hinder your efforts to succeed.

Ultimately, your attitude affects your outcome. If you focus on finding an agent, and if you believe you can accomplish this goal, you find opportunities to contact agents everywhere. If you don't believe it's possible to work with an agent, the process feels difficult and locating agents seems a struggle.

Compelling scientific studies suggest that consciousness affects the outside world; in other words,

people can direct reality with their minds. Quantum physics has shown that when you observe an object, it is affected by the fact that you trained your attention on it. Also, double-slit experiments performed in high school science labs demonstrate that how you observe matter and energy changes the way both behave. These experiments provide evidence that our minds—or where we place our focus—affect the physical world. Therefore, it makes sense that if we focus on what we want to create, we have a higher likelihood of manifesting it.

Deliberate creation makes sense in light of recent brain imaging studies, too. Scientists found neurons in monkeys and humans that mirror the behavior of someone being observed. When you observe a person's action, the same pattern of brain activation that allows that person to do what they are doing (e.g., writing) is mirrored in your brain. Also, the regions of the brain that prepare the body for movement and attention are activated, even though you aren't actively behaving in the same manner. The human brain automatically mimics the actions of another person.

This explains why you may feel inspired and excited when you hear a successful author speak or see one signing books. It stimulates your brain into feeling as if you are onstage speaking or signing your published book, which helps you embody and create that same experience.

Keep in mind that your brain can't distinguish between a physical or mental experience. That's why athletes use visualization and conscious creation. For example, a runner might visualize herself running a race. She feels the ease with which she moves and the tiredness in her muscles when she gets to the halfway mark. She imagines pushing through fatigue, running faster, and crossing the finish line. She experiences the exhilaration and sense of accomplishment from completing—and winning—the race. As she imagines these things, her brain causes her muscles to react in a manner similar to physically running. The runner's brain and body record the experience as if it were real. The mental and muscle memories help her bring that identical experience into physical reality the next time she runs a race.

As you visualize yourself moving through the stages of idea and career creation, your mind and body record the images as real events. When you set the intention to succeed—to win your race to a successful writing career or authorship—you activate the action centers in your brain. This supports your efforts to do something physical to make your vision real.

The Power of This Book

What do these ideas about the brain have to do with reading and using this book? This interactive guide is your self-exploration, ideation, manifestation, goal-setting, creativity, affirmation, focus, and visioning journal to help you bring your projects and career to fruition. It incorporates:

- both sides of your brain
- writing
- drawing, coloring, and colors
- your thoughts and feelings
- visualization
- affirmations
- goal and intention setting
- your ability to change

The intention of the exercises in this book is to inspire you to create what you most desire. Creation, however, can take time. Set aside at least a few minutes each day to work with this guide, and pick it up when inspiration strikes or when you need inspiration. It can help you with focus, clarity, motivation, courage, relaxation, confidence, and progress toward new habits, thoughts, and objectives. Use it every time you want to develop a new idea, achieve a goal, or realize a dream related to your writing.

To reach a new and sustainable level of success, commit at least forty days to your creative visualization practice. In that amount of time, you can create a reward pathway in your brain for your new mental and creative behaviors. When you visualize a goal or idea, and see and feel it achieved or created, your brain records this as a positive stimulus. Additionally, if you take action toward achieving that goal, which increases your confidence, your brain registers this as a reward. These rewarding stimuli then serve as important motivators for future behavior. When the reward pathway in your brain gets activated, it encourages you to repeat the behaviors, actions, thoughts, or feelings that caused that response.

The more often you experience pleasure or reward from working with the exercises in this book, the more quickly and easily your brain records this fact and helps you form a creative and success-driven habit. That's why it's important to commit—and intend—to use this book for forty days. In that period of time, you can change your way of looking at yourself and your projects, as well as your ability to make your creative dreams a reality. You'll also set creation in motion.

Creative Visualization for Writers is divided into five sections based on what you might need or want at any given time:

1. **SELF-EXPLORATION:** exercises and prompts to help you look at yourself in relationship to your creative goals and dreams
2. **GOALS:** exercises and prompts to help you clarify and set goals
3. **CREATIVITY:** exercises and prompts to inspire your creative impulses
4. **VISUALIZATION:** exercises and prompts to help you visualize ideas, dreams, and goals
5. **FOCUS:** pages to color for relaxation and visualization, and affirmations paired with coloring book pages to help you manage your attention

You may not want to complete every section or every exercise in a particular section. Feel free to pick and choose. For example, you may want to focus on the Goals section if you need to set intentions, or spend time with the Creativity section if you want to develop ideas or stimulate your muse. Use the coloring pages when you want to relax or focus. Use the affirmations when you are ready to commit to changing a particular negative thought. The Self-Evaluation section helps you learn more about what hinders or facilitates your writing goals and dreams. You also can work with the book from start to finish.

This book is not meant to be a one-time read. Return to its pages whenever you need inspiration, relaxation, or a creative boost. Allow it to become your companion—a supportive friend to help you bring your ideas into the world and keep you motivated and courageous.

Use this book to become a visionary, keep your vision alive, and make it real.

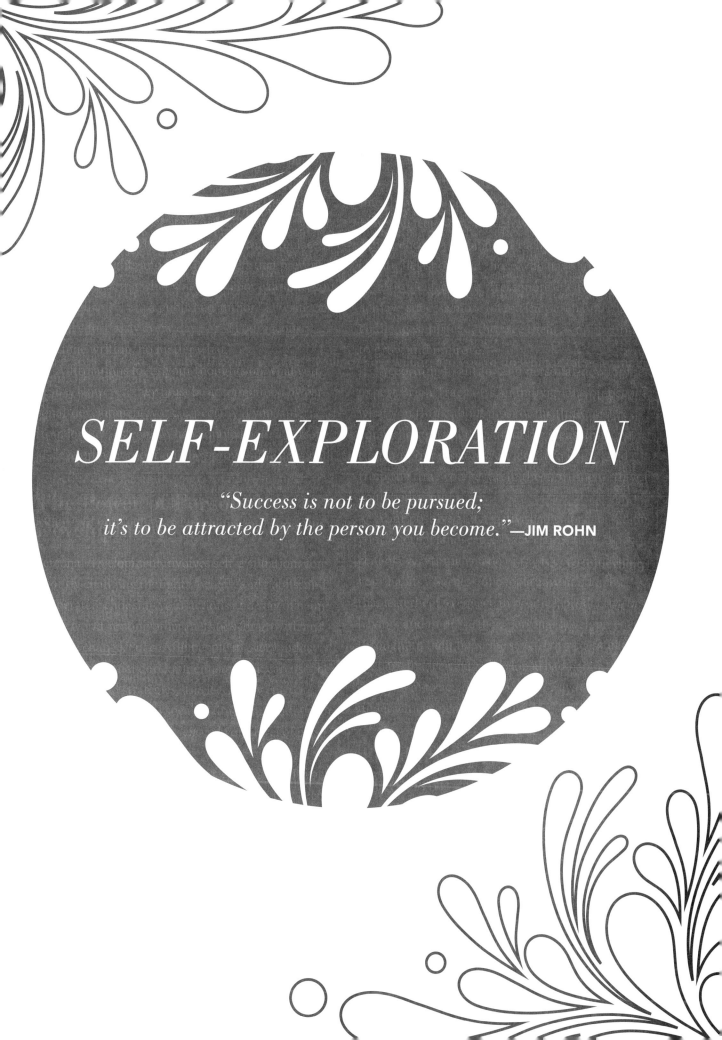

SELF-EXPLORATION

"Success is not to be pursued;
it's to be attracted by the person you become."—**JIM ROHN**

Do You Know Yourself?

Look in the mirror. Do you see someone familiar or unfamiliar? Is the face that looks back at you a person whom you can count on to help you get where you want to go? Or does that person hinder your progress toward your goals and dreams?

You need to become well acquainted with yourself if you want to succeed in any endeavor. And you must be honest about how and what you need to change to achieve your goals. The better you know yourself, the easier it becomes to make your writing dreams real and create a career as a successful author.

You've got to know—and to a great extent, control—your mind. To accomplish this, you can do the following:

- Identify what beliefs and thoughts stop you from (or help you start) taking action.
- Evaluate what habits make it difficult (or easy) to fulfill your potential and purpose.
- Determine the character traits that help or hurt your progress toward realizing your writing dream.

This knowledge gives you the power to break through obstacles that prevent you from becoming a writer or author, increase your level of success, or create an amazing career. It helps you choose to be the kind of person who succeeds, a person who doesn't dwell on negative and unsupportive thoughts and fears and doesn't continue practicing self-defeating behaviors. Then you can focus on thoughts, beliefs, feelings, and habits that support you on your journey to success.

Look yourself in the eyes, and begin the exploration.

What Do You Question?

Is your work, career, or life plagued by question marks? Questions can mire your progress by making you feel insecure or causing you to focus on the worst possible potential outcome.

Questions also are necessary. They help you determine the worth of a project or if taking a step in a new direction will get you where you want to go.

Questions move you forward. They help you gain new information, including details about yourself and how you need to change and improve to succeed as a writer.

Color in the question mark below as you think about the following questions. Then answer them.

In what ways do you question yourself? For example, do you question your writing skill, your ability to complete a book, or the validity of your ideas? Why?

Is a question stopping you from creating the career of your dreams? What is it?

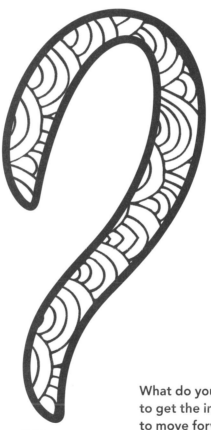

What questions do you have about a new idea or project you want to start?

What do you need to ask yourself to get the information necessary to move forward?

Where Do You Pause?

Commas create a pause in the stream of writing. Sometimes, on your way to achieving your goals, you need to pause. And sometimes you pause without cause.

You want to move forward with your writing idea, project, or career—and you plan to keep moving forward. Yet you pause. Why?

Maybe you need time off or a chance to appreciate your progress before taking the next step. Maybe you pause because you have a question about yourself, your idea, or your ability. Or you run up against a problem for which you don't yet have a solution. Perhaps you just don't feel like moving forward at that moment. Admit it: Watching television, reading a novel, or spending time with friends and family just seems, well, easier.

As you color in the comma below, think about the following questions. Then write down your answers.

Why are you pausing?

Where, and in what ways, are you pausing in your life, career, or work? Why?

What projects have you paused and never restarted? Why?

Do you need (or want) to pause? Why?

Where Do You Stop?

A period marks a full stop at the end of a sentence. Do you feel like you've stopped acting on your ideas or making progress toward your writing career?

Any number of factors might stop you: a lack of self-confidence, fear, the need for more money, other people's judgments, or laziness, for example.

As you color in the period below, think about where you have stopped, even though you'd like to make progress in your journey to become a successful writer. Then answer the questions below.

Where have you come to a full stop in your progress toward becoming a writer or bringing an idea to life?

Why did you stop? Is something blocking your path?

Is the period (obstacle) real, a figment of your imagination, or a future possibility? Be honest!

What Excites You?

Exclamation points symbolize impact and excitement in your prose. Does your writing career or current writing project make you feel as if you are living an exclamation point? Or do you feel dispassionate and bored regarding your work?

Color in the exclamation point below, and consider the questions on this page.

What project most excites you right now? Why?

What idea, project, or aspect of your career offers you the largest opportunity to make an impact on the world or on your readers' lives? Why?

What aspects of your career do you feel most passionate about? Why?

How would you physically express your excitement for writing? Draw yourself in action, whatever that action may be.

Then get moving. Dance, yell, run in circles—whatever shows the world your excitement and passion. Be an exclamation point!

Can You Commit?

The word *commitment* sometimes carries a negative connotation. You've heard people say, "He won't commit" or "She's a commitment-phobe" in a judgmental tone. You probably cringe when someone enlists your involvement by asking, "Will you commit?"

You need to attach a positive feeling to commitment—and a large desire to commit—when it comes to your ideas, work, and career. If you aren't committed, no one else will be either. Without commitment, you won't take the necessary steps to realize your dreams.

How committed are you to writing, your current projects and ideas, or your career? Why?

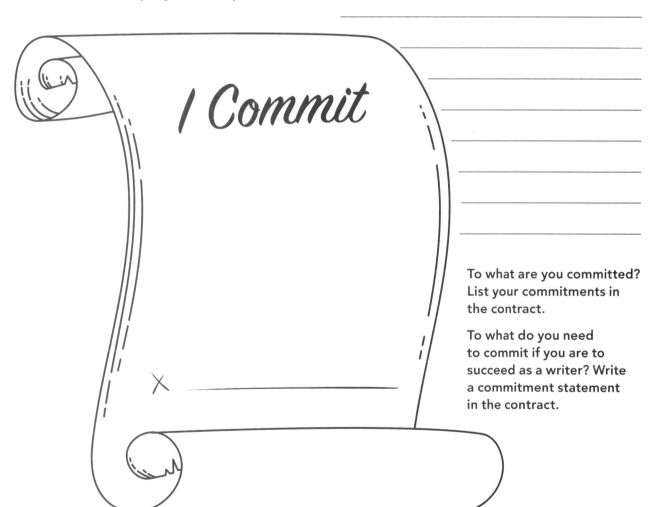

I Commit

X _____

To what are you committed? List your commitments in the contract.

To what do you need to commit if you are to succeed as a writer? Write a commitment statement in the contract.

Are You Willing to Succeed?

To develop a career as a successful author—or to develop even just one successful book—you must do more than write. You have to build an author platform. To do that, you must get involved with social networking, build an e-mail list, speak at conferences and events, create a website and blog, promote your book, and learn how to run a business. You have to wear a promoter's hat, an entrepreneur's hat, a blogger's hat, a techie's hat, and a speaker's hat, as well as a writer's hat.

Answer these three crucial questions:

1. Are you willing to be more than a writer? Why or why not?

_____

_____

_____

_____

_____

2. Are you willing to do what it takes—whatever it takes—to achieve your goals? Why or why not?

_____

_____

_____

_____

_____

3. Are you willing to fail? Why or why not?

_____

_____

_____

_____

_____

Successful writers, authors, and self-publishers possess a willingness to do whatever it takes to achieve their goals, but they are *unwilling* to fail. They are willing to sacrifice—sleep, money, free time, whatever—to reach their goal. Are you?

They are willing to try, even if their effort ends up looking like failure. They don't see the outcome as failure but rather as a learning experience that helps them get closer to their goal. They try again.

Becoming a successful writer takes a ton of willingness.

On a scale of 1 to 10, with 10 being the most willing, how willing are you to do what it takes to make your dreams real? Why?

| 1 | 2 | 3 | 4 | 5 | 6 | 7 | 8 | 9 | 10 |

_____

_____

_____

What are you willing or unwilling to do to achieve your creative writing goals? Why?

_____

_____

_____

How do your decisions affect your ability to succeed? Evaluate this by filling in the two lists below.

What are you willing to do to achieve your creative goals?

Yes! I am willing to …	No! I am not willing to …

Yes!

Put on Magic Glasses

You may have heard the adage "To truly understand another person, you must walk a mile in her shoes." This lesson has more to do with objectively viewing someone's life and experiences than literally getting a feel for their penny loafers or heels.

Try this advice instead: See through someone else's eyes. Imagine putting on a pair of magic glasses—no, not rose-colored glasses!—and seeing from an acquisitions editor's perspective.

As the person responsible for acquiring manuscripts for a publishing company, an acquisitions editor has the knowledge and experience to know which book ideas represent potential bestsellers, or at least which projects might make a profit for the publisher.

No matter how you plan to publish, to succeed as an author, you must see yourself and your ideas through an acquisitions editor's eyes. Likewise, if you write articles and essays, you must see yourself and your article ideas through a publication editor's eyes.

Doing so takes objectivity. The publishing process requires objectivity in many situations, such as when you evaluate your idea, work with an editor or designer, or read reviews of your work.

Are you objective? Why or why not?

_____

_____

_____

_____

_____

Can you look at your work through an editor's eyes? Why or why not?

_____

_____

_____

_____

_____

How could you become more objective?

_____

_____

_____

_____

_____

_____

How can you learn to truly hear and take action on constructive criticism?

_____

_____

_____

_____

_____

_____

Is Your Glass Half Empty or Half Full?

Your worldview affects what you create. If you have a glass-half-empty perspective, you see the world from a pessimistic point of view. If you have a glass-half-full (or overflowing) perspective, you see it from an optimistic point of view. Optimists create more of what they desire than pessimists because they don't let judgments, criticism, or rejection distract or hinder them. They don't take these things personally. Instead, they see so-called negative events as opportunities for self-improvement or challenges to better their work. And they jump at the chance to do both, which is why they succeed. Answer these questions:

Are you an optimist with a glass-half-full perspective or a pessimist with a glass-half-empty perspective? How do you know?

_____

_____

_____

_____

_____

_____

_____

How does your perspective help or hinder your efforts to achieve your goals?

_____

_____

_____

_____

_____

_____

_____

What one thing could you do today to change or enhance your worldview so you can manifest your desires and realize your dreams? Write about it below.

_____

_____

_____

_____

_____

_____

_____

Color in the glass that best represents the worldview you want to have.

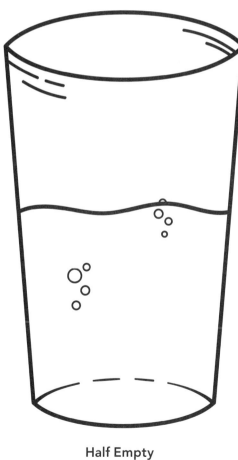

Half Empty

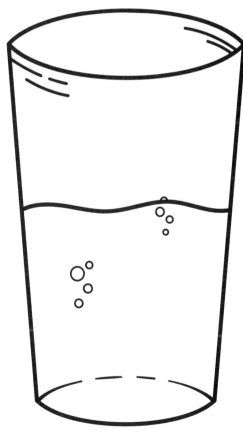

Half Full

Are You Ready to Give Up?

Many authors, actors, artists, and songwriters claim that it takes fifteen to twenty years to become an "overnight success." They are right. You've heard stories of authors selling millions of copies of their first book, but that is exceedingly rare, and most devote years of hard work prior to achieving that result.

You might feel as if you must climb a huge mountain before you can put a stake in the ground claiming you've reached the summit of your writing goal.

You may believe that scaling the mountain is just too difficult and want to give up.

The writers and authors who succeed are tenacious. They are determined to succeed. Nothing stops them. They refuse to fail.

Find out if you are willing and able to carry the flag of tenacity to the top of the mountain. Answer these questions:

Are you willing to do whatever it takes to reach your destination? Why or why not?

_____

_____

_____

_____

_____

_____

_____

What makes you feel like giving up? Why?

_____

_____

_____

_____

_____

_____

_____

How can you overcome those feelings and take another step forward?

_____

_____

_____

_____

_____

_____

What one thing could you do to develop more tenacity?

_____

_____

_____

_____

_____

_____

Do You Have an Author Attitude?

Many successful writers and authors share a particular attitude. If you have all four of the following characteristics, you've got an Author Attitude, too:

- ☐ **W**illingness
- ☐ **O**ptimism
- ☐ **O**bjectivity
- ☐ **T**enacity

W
O
O
T

Willingness
↓
Optimism
↓
Objectivity
↓
Tenacity

Based on your responses in the last four exercises, check off the characteristics you possess.

Do you have an Author Attitude? Why or why not?

_____

_____

_____

_____

What do you need to do to generate one? Journal about this below.

_____

_____

_____

_____

_____

_____

_____

_____

WOOT!
WOOT!
Woot!
WOOT!

Do You Have Passion?

Passion flows *generally* between you and your writing, and *specifically* between you and your current project. You feel passionate about your work—or you should.

Lack of passion stops the flow of your work and keeps you stuck in place, much like a period at the end of a sentence. Without passion, you may not write at all.

If you write about topics that don't interest you, you'll find it difficult to generate passion for your project. So write about your passions. Develop passion projects! Keep passion at the forefront of what you create. Answer these questions:

Does your work sync up with your passion? How?

_____

_____

_____

_____

_____

_____

What are you passionate about? List the subjects, hobbies, activities, or causes about which you feel passionate. Why are you passionate about them?

_____

_____

_____

_____

_____

_____

_____

How can you incorporate those passions into your written work?

_____

_____

_____

_____

_____

How can you build a writing career around your passions?

_____

_____

_____

_____

_____

Now go write with passion!

What's Your Big Why?

Do you know why you want to write your essay, article, blog, or book? What do you hope to accomplish?

The reason you write provides your purpose, mission, or calling—what I like to call the *Big Why*. It keeps you writing day in and day out, no matter what, and doesn't allow you to give up or fail.

What is your Big Why?

_____

_____

_____

_____

Do you have a purpose, mission, or calling? Describe it.

_____

_____

_____

_____

Write a mission or purpose statement below. For example: "I feel compelled to write this book because …"

_____

_____

_____

_____

Create a plaque or poster that states your mission. Place it in your office or workspace.

Big Why

Are You Inspired?

When you combine passion for what you write with purpose for your work and career, you feel inspired. It's like you've touched a match to a firecracker—get ready for the explosion!

Inspiration leads you to take action. You won't complete tasks because you feel you *should*; you'll do so because you *must*. You'll know it's the right next step for you, your work, and your career. And you'll *want* to take action immediately.

You can get inspired in other ways, such as by beginning your project. Writing inspires more writing. Or you can change your workspace or work location, or make your office a sacred space. Make sure the place where you work inspires you. (See the Creativity section for more on this topic.)

Reading inspiring books and hanging out with inspiring people or writers helps, too!

Evaluate your level of inspiration:

On a scale from 1 to 10, with 10 being the highest, how inspired do you feel by your work?

1	2	3	4	5	6	7	8	9	10

On a scale from 1 to 10, with 10 being the highest, how passionate do you feel about your subject matter?

1	2	3	4	5	6	7	8	9	10

Is your work purposeful? In what way?

_____

_____

_____

_____

What could you do to light a fire under yourself and your work?

_____

_____

_____

_____

_____

What inspires you most about your ideas, projects, and writing career? Why?

_____

_____

_____

_____

_____

What Do You Value?

It's important to know what you value or deem important. When your work reflects your values, it feeds your purpose and passion. It keeps you interested and inspired.

When your career revolves around your values, your authenticity shines through every product or service you provide, including your articles, essays, blog posts, and books. Values work like beacons that attract readers, customers, and clients.

Make a list of your top five values, such as friendship, family, honesty, self-care, and service.

1. _____

2. _____

3. _____

4. _____

5. _____

Does your work express your values? How?

_____

_____

_____

_____

_____

_____

Do your values run through your work in the form of topics or themes? Describe how.

_____

_____

_____

_____

_____

_____

How could you incorporate your values into your work or career?

_____

_____

_____

_____

_____

_____

_____

_____

_____

_____

_____

_____

_____

Do You Take Action?

Think about your writing journey in terms of running a race. What's your starting-line behavior? When the starting gun fires, do you run as fast as you can, lag behind after a slow start, or cower and slink off to the locker room? When you get an idea, or know it's time to begin a task that moves your work or career forward, do you take action?

It's okay to mull over your idea and evaluate its viability—but not for months or years. Procrastination never helped anyone become a successful writer.

What makes you take action? Why?

_____

_____

_____

_____

What stops you from taking action? Why?

_____

_____

_____

_____

How can you get yourself to take action when you become immobile?

_____

_____

_____

_____

Do you take inspired action—action inspired by purpose combined with passion? How?

_____

_____

_____

_____

How can you ensure you take action when necessary?

_____

_____

_____

_____

What do you need to take action on immediately?

_____

_____

_____

_____

Take action now!

Do You Have Reasons or Results?

If you aren't taking action, you must have a reason. But that reason probably isn't helping you get the results you desire.

You can have reasons or results. The choice is yours. If you want results, drop the reasons why you aren't taking action.

Actions I Need to Take to Get Results	Reasons I'm Not Taking Action

Actions I've Taken/Date	Results Achieved

Who Do You Want to Become?

Your life is like a canvas upon which you can paint. You can create the frame for that canvas with your negative thoughts and beliefs, unsupportive habits, or unhelpful personality traits. Or you can frame your vision of who you can become and what you can do in the world with positivity.

Expand the borders of your canvas with your positive thoughts, supportive habits, and unlimited beliefs. Paint a picture by imagining your best writing self and your dream writing career or life. What characteristics would you need to possess? How would you describe yourself and your career?

As best-selling author and high-performance coach Brendon Burchard says, "You have a clean slate every day you wake up. You have a chance every single morning to make that change and be the person you want to be. You just have to decide to do it. Decide today is the day; this is going to be my day."

On the canvas, draw a picture of the person you want to become. Keep that image in front of you daily. Take a picture of it and put in your phone, use it as your computer's background, or print it out, frame it, and keep it on your desk. You can even add an affirmation to it, such as "I am now published and making a living as a writer."

Or describe your future self. Keep that description in a place you can access it daily—such as on your bathroom mirror or in your phone's notes section.

How Do You Want to Be Known?

Brands aren't just for big-box stores like Walmart and Best Buy or manufacturers like Nike, Audi, and Rolex. Writers and authors benefit from branding as well.

To find your brand, answer this important question:

How do you want to be known as an author or writer?

_____

_____

Answering the following questions also helps you define your brand:

What do you stand for as a writer and human being? Why?

_____

_____

What topics and themes do you write about? Why?

_____

_____

What benefit or value do you provide to your readers?

_____

_____

Your name is a brand, but it has to mean something to people. Use it as the URL and name of your author website, as I do with ninaamir.com. Or give your site a branded name, like howtoblogabook.com or writenonfictionnow.com.

Follow your site name with a tagline. What short phrase would you include after your name? For example, I'm known by my name, Nina Amir, and I'm called "the Inspiration to Creation Coach." The benefit I offer is in my tagline. I help people "**A**chieve **M**ore **I**nspired **R**esults," and this acronym pulls together my brand.

What Part of Yourself Best Serves You?

Research shows that your inner voice either helps or hinders your ability to achieve goals. The affirmation "I can do it" keeps you moving forward if you are a courageous person, but if your inner voice is fearful, you'll balk at taking that first step.

Your "self" is comprised of many "selves." By this, I don't mean that you have multiple personalities but numerous energetic parts that live within you and influence your life. They affect your decisions, emotions, thoughts, behaviors, relationships, and whether you achieve your goals and create your dreams.

Do you know your inner selves? Do you know what parts of yourself help you ideate, create, write, complete, or sell your work? Name them.

_____

_____

_____

What parts serve you best when it comes to building your career? Why?

_____

_____

_____

Can you figure out which ones help you move forward and which ones hold you back?

_____

_____

_____

Your Inner Child

Your Inner Child thinks, feels, responds, and sees the world the way you did when you were young. This self still carries the same fears and beliefs you held then.

Your Inner Child needs protection; the adult "you" provides it. But the Inner Child also needs to be reassured that you know best. As the adult, it is up to you to make informed decisions that don't hurt your Inner Child.

Often, your Inner Child feels scared, unsure, lonely, sad, or some other negative emotion that keeps you stuck. Other times, your Inner Child is playful, happy, excited, eager to move forward, and filled with positive energy to keep you going.

Ask your Inner Child the questions below. Write the responses with your nondominant hand. Doing so helps you access this younger self who was not yet a proficient scribe.

How old are you? _____

What makes you fearful? Why?

_____

_____

What makes you happy? Why?

_____

_____

How can I make you feel safe?

_____

_____

Do you like to write? Why or why not?

_____

_____

What ideas do you have that you wish I would act on?

_____

_____

How do you feel right now?

_____

_____

Now draw what you imagine your Inner Child looks like below.

Your Inner Successful Author

Your Inner Successful Author knows you can succeed and, in fact, feels frustrated that you haven't gotten with the program and achieved success already. After all, this part of you already feels successful. Call upon this self when you need advice, support, or information about your next steps toward your goals.

Ask your Inner Successful Author the questions below. Then close your eyes, and allow this self to answer. If you want, ask each question from one chair—yours—and then move to another chair where you imagine your Inner Successful Author sits. Then, using your dominant hand, write the answers.

Which one of my ideas should I pursue? Why?

_____

_____

What publishing path should I take? Why?

_____

_____

What action will move me forward most quickly toward successful publishing? Why?

_____

_____

What tips do you have for me at this time?

_____

_____

What other advice or information do I need from you right now?

_____

_____

Now draw what you imagine your Inner Successful Author looks like.

Your Inner Sales Rep

Your Inner Sales Rep loves promotion and marketing. This self's preferred activity is selling, and it sees no conflict between art and commerce.

Call upon this self when you need to pre-promote your book by building your author platform. This "you" is happy to help attract a fan base or do whatever it takes to build your mailing list or social-network following. This is the self you want in full force when you release your book, as it will gladly assist you with marketing.

If you want good ideas about how to promote yourself and your work, talk to your Inner Sales Rep. And when you feel uncomfortable pitching your work or encouraging potential readers to buy your book, invoke the energy of this self.

Ask your Inner Sales Rep the following questions. Let this self answer in the same way your Inner Successful Author replied to your queries, using the instructions on the previous pages.

How do I best build an author platform?

_____

_____

What promotion or marketing techniques would I enjoy most? Why?

_____

_____

What promotion or marketing techniques would work best for me and my books? Why?

_____

_____

What is the one thing I can do right now that will help me build a platform quickly? Why?

_____

_____

What is the one thing I can do right now that will help me sell the most books?

_____

_____

What tips do you have for me at this time?

_____

_____

Now draw what you imagine your Inner Sales Rep looks like below.

Your Inner Businessperson

As you navigate the complexities of publishing, you'll find your Inner Businessperson quite useful. Most writers hate the business aspect of, well, their business. So call on your Inner Businessperson for help and advice by asking this self the questions below. Let this self answer in the same way your Inner Successful Author and Inner Sales Rep replied to your queries, using the instructions on the previous pages.

How can I make my idea more marketable?

_____

_____

How can I best describe my experience and expertise?

_____

_____

What skills do I need to manage my self-publishing team?

_____

_____

How can I be a better businessperson?

_____

_____

How can I make myself more attractive as a publishing partner?

_____

_____

Now draw what you imagine your Inner Businessperson looks like below.

Your Inner Writer

Your Inner Writer serves as your muse and task-master. This self provides inspiration and ideas, and drives you to sit down at the computer and write.

If you aren't writing or lack inspiration, call on your Inner Writer. You'll start producing work in no time.

Ask your Inner Writer the questions below. Use your dominant hand. Let this self answer in the same way your Inner Successful Author, Inner Sales Rep, and Inner Businessperson replied to your queries, using the instructions on the previous pages.

How can I produce more words per day?

_____

_____

What one ritual could I create to inspire my writing every day? How or why will it help me?

_____

_____

What ideas do you have for my next article or book?

_____

_____

How can I become a more productive writer?

_____

_____

When is the best time for me to write? Why?

_____

_____

Now draw what you imagine your Inner Writer looks like below.

Do You Pat Yourself on the Back?

When was the last time you wrote down all the great things you've done, the goals you've achieved, or the challenges you've gracefully and successfully tackled?

It's time to do that.

Acknowledge yourself. Make a list of your accomplishments over the last twelve months:

_____   _____

_____   _____

_____   _____

_____   _____

_____   _____

_____   _____

Now, reach around and pat yourself on the back. Better yet, go celebrate!

How will you celebrate? For instance, will you eat dinner or ice cream with a friend, go to a movie, take a bath, or sit on the beach and read? Draw the celebration below.

Give Yourself a Star!

Remember when you used to receive little gold stars for accomplishing something in school? It's important to tell yourself you are great, special, good at writing, honest, loving or lovable, or any other positive word you feel describes you well.

Award yourself a gold star just for being you.

Write your name in the middle of the star below. Then use an adjective or phrase to describe yourself, such as "I am successful," "I am an author," "I am published," "I am conscientious," or "I am a great ideator."

Starting a sentence with "I am …" holds an enormous amount of creative power. Use it to help you become the person you want to be.

Tear this page out, and hang it where you can see it.

Now go buy some gold, silver, and colored star stickers, and award them to yourself daily!

Do You Have Clarity?

For writers, clarity is like a two-way street. When you travel in one direction, you focus on your message being easily understood, seen, heard, or read. That means you must clearly express yourself so people understand and remember your missive.

When you travel in the opposite direction, you focus on understanding your subject matter and story, as well as yourself, your goals, and your purpose. Otherwise, you can't express yourself with clarity.

What's your message? Carefully write it below.

_____

_____

_____

_____

In what area of your work or career do you have the most clarity?

_____

_____

_____

_____

In what area of your work or career do you need more clarity?

_____

_____

_____

_____

What Do You Know for Sure?

Oprah Winfrey often begins sentences with the phrase "What I know for sure ..." when she is going to share something she's learned. Now it's your turn.

What do you know for sure? Do you know that your book or article idea targets your market, that you can write a book, or that you have a big enough platform to attract a publisher, for example? Make a list of those things below. Write a paragraph or short essay about each one.

What I know for sure ...

_____

_____

_____

_____

_____

_____

What I know for sure ...

_____

_____

_____

_____

_____

_____

What I know for sure ...

_____

_____

_____

_____

_____

_____

_____

Do You Have an Alice Attitude?

Without clarity, you wander. This is the long way to get anywhere, including to your writing destination.

With clarity, you walk a straight and purposeful path. This is the shortest way to get where you want to go.

In Lewis Carroll's *Alice's Adventures in Wonderland*, Alice and the Cheshire Cat have the following conversation:

> **ALICE:** Would you tell me, please, which way I ought to go from here?
> **THE CHESHIRE CAT:** That depends a good deal on where you want to get to.
> **ALICE:** I don't much care where.
> **THE CHESHIRE CAT:** Then it doesn't much matter which way you go.
> **ALICE:** … so long as I get somewhere.
> **THE CHESHIRE CAT:** Oh, you're sure to do that, if only you walk long enough.

Don't have an Alice Attitude—pick a destination! Is it successful authorship, published authorship, a writing business, or somewhere else? Name it, and then describe it below.

MY DESTINATION: _____

_____

_____

_____

_____

What does this destination look like? Draw it!

Are Your Thoughts Negative or Positive?

What you focus on expands. If you constantly think about what's going wrong with your writing projects and career, this negative attitude generates more of the same. If you focus on what's working and going well, positive results grow from your positive viewpoint.

Spend a day or two becoming conscious of your thoughts. Then make a list of the negative ones.

Now, turn your negative thoughts into affirmations. For example, if you often think, *No one reads my blog posts*, create an affirmation like "My blog posts provide great value and, therefore, are read and appreciated by many people every day." If you think, *It's hard to find an agent*, turn that thought into an affirmation like "I will have an easy time finding an agent because my ideas and my writing are worth publishing."

Once you have crafted your affirmations, cross out your old negative thoughts. Say, "Negative thoughts, be gone!" as you draw a line through each one. You've just traded negativity for positivity.

NEGATIVE THOUGHT: _____

AFFIRMATION: _____

NEGATIVE THOUGHT: _____

AFFIRMATION: _____

NEGATIVE THOUGHT: _____

AFFIRMATION: _____

NEGATIVE THOUGHT: _____

AFFIRMATION: _____

NEGATIVE THOUGHT: _____

AFFIRMATION: _____

NEGATIVE THOUGHT: _____

AFFIRMATION: _____

NEGATIVE THOUGHT: _____

AFFIRMATION: _____

NEGATIVE THOUGHT: _____

AFFIRMATION: _____

If you find yourself saying or thinking something negative, qualify the statement with these two word: *until recently*. Here is an example: "I've never made money from my writing … *until recently*." Immediately transform your negative thought into a positive one, and start creating exactly what you want rather than what you don't.

You also can add the word *yet* to the end of a sentence to change it from negative to positive. For example, "I haven't found an agent … *yet*."

To help you remember and repeat your affirmations, type them into your smartphone as a reminder, perhaps even programming them as alarms. Or use an affirmation app for your phone: Record, and then listen daily.

Negative thoughts, be gone!

What Do You Believe?

A thought you think once remains just a thought. A recurring thought becomes a belief.

Do you have negative thoughts that have turned into unsupportive beliefs, such as "I'm not good enough," "I don't write well enough," "I'm not a good businessperson," or "I can't do it"? Do you believe literary agents don't want to say yes, self-publishing is hard, traditional publishers can't be trusted, you have to know someone to break into a magazine, or authors are always poor?

These beliefs don't serve you or your dream of turning your ideas into written products or creating a career as a writer.

Below, list your beliefs about yourself, your ability to become a successful writer, and publishing in general. Then put a mark next to the negative beliefs you need to change. How will you change them? Change your negative thoughts into positive affirmations. (See the "Are Your Thoughts Negative or Positive?" exercise and the Focus section for help.)

I believe ...

_____

_____

_____

_____

_____

_____

My New Affirmations

_____

_____

_____

_____

_____

_____

Are You Courageous?

Anxiety, worry, and fear keep you from realizing your dreams and achieving your goals. They serve as jailers that imprison you in your current level of success and make it impossible for you to move forward or level up.

You need courage to break out of your cell. The more daring you become, the more quickly you move through and past the things that cause you trepidation. To conquer anxiety, worry, or fear, question whatever brings up that emotion.

Make a list of things that cause you worry or anxiety:

_____   _____

_____   _____

_____   _____

_____   _____

Then answer the following questions:

Why do these things make me afraid?

_____

_____

_____

Does the experience or thing I fear exist in my life now, or is it only a potential reality that may never occur?

_____

_____

_____

Not all fears are based in reality. That's why fear has been defined as *False Evidence Appearing Real.* Again, do you have a reason *now* to be afraid, or are you focusing on a potentiality?

Don't waste your time and energy on potential outcomes you might never experience and that you don't want to bring into your life. Instead, focus on what you do want and on how to create it.

How can you act bravely? What three daring things could you do to move your writing career forward quickly? List them below.

1. _____

2. _____

3. _____

According to keynote concert performer Tiamo De Vettori, "Fear is the only thing that gets smaller the faster you run toward it." Choose a fear. Picture yourself running toward it right now. Draw yourself moving through this fear or making it smaller below.

Do You Produce Work Consistently?

Writers write. A productive writer produces work and, as Seth Godin likes to say, ships that work. She completes the project. She gets the manuscript out the door so it gets published and people read it.

On a scale of 1 to 10, with 10 being the highest, how productive are you? (Be honest.)

1   2   3   4   5   6   7   8   9   10

Do you write consistently? Why or why not?

_____

_____

On a scale of 1 to 10, with 10 being the highest, how productive are you?

1   2   3   4   5   6   7   8   9   10

How would you accomplish the highest level of productivity?

_____

_____

Create a writing schedule below that you are willing to stick to and that you know you can keep.

	Monday	Tuesday	Wednesday	Thursday	Friday	Saturday	Sunday
5 A.M.							
6 A.M.							
7 A.M.							
8 A.M.							
9 A.M.							
10 A.M.							
11 A.M.							
12 P.M.							
1 P.M.							
2 P.M.							
3 P.M.							
4 P.M.							
5 P.M.							
6 P.M.							
7 P.M.							
8 P.M.							

Do You Manage Your Attention?

You may think your productivity hinges on how you manage your time, but it doesn't. You can't manage time. You have twenty-four hours per day and seven days per week. That's it.

However, you can manage your attention during your writing time to become more productive.

What distracts you most during your writing time? Why?

_____

_____

_____

How could you eliminate those distractions?

_____

_____

_____

Draw a picture of yourself crushing your distractions. Then draw the result of managing your attention.

Do You Know Your Weaknesses?

You may have been advised in the past to focus on your weaknesses. Proponents of this strategy believe that by turning weaknesses into strengths, you achieve success.

Here's the rub: No matter how hard you try, those weak spots often remain weak. By focusing on them, you magnify them, which increases your self-doubt and lowers your self-esteem and confidence. The more attention you pay to your weaknesses, the weaker you seem.

In some cases, your weaknesses are so ingrained in your nature that working on them becomes detrimental to success. For instance, you might be a disorganized person. You can work at becoming organized, but you may fall back to disorganized habits regularly. You'd be better off putting your attention on something you are able to change.

Stop magnifying your weaknesses. Instead, recognize them, and find ways to get help in those areas. For example, enlist an office manager or virtual assistant to help you stay organized. Let others who possess stronger skills in grammar, tax filing, book cover design, social media—or any area in which you feel weak—handle that aspect of your work or life. Like a president, surround yourself with cabinet members (a team) to help you in areas where you need it most.

List your weaknesses below. For each weakness, devise a way to get support in that area. Then ask for it!

Weakness	Support

Focus on Your Strengths

Brendon Burchard says, "Amplifying what is great within you will accelerate your life faster than fixing what you think 'limits' you." Indeed, your strengths historically helped you achieve success. They have served you well and continue to do so.

Focus on your strengths rather than your weaknesses. Create more of what's working and less of what isn't!

List your strengths below. For each strength, list three ways you could put it to better use to make your writing dreams real.

Strength	Way to Use It

Now do some weightlifting to build those strengths!

Do You Follow Success Clues?

To solve the riddle of writing success, you must actively look for and find success clues. To do so:

1. Study successful writers, authors, bloggers, or journalists. Determine how they became successful. Can you model their actions, habits, attitudes, and so on?
2. Study your own success. What steps did you take to succeed? Can you repeat those steps again or in other situations?

Find success clues by asking the following questions:

Who are your role models and heroes? Why?

_____

_____

_____

_____

_____

How can you emulate their success?

_____

_____

_____

_____

_____

What habits do other successful writers have that you can adopt?

_____

_____

_____

_____

_____

What successful habits do you have?

_____

_____

_____

_____

_____

When you achieved success in the past, how did you do so? How can you repeat that behavior?

_____

_____

_____

_____

_____

What Has Failure Taught You?

Failure also leaves clues. Take time to examine your failures and learn from them. As Napoleon Hill says, "The primary reason for failure is that people do not develop new plans to replace the plans that didn't work." You have ample chances to create new plans in this book. (See the Goals section for more.) Now, journal on the following topics:

My biggest failures were:

_____

_____

_____

_____

_____

I learned the following things from my failures:

_____

_____

_____

_____

_____

I will do the following things differently in the future:

_____

_____

_____

_____

_____

What Are Your Payoffs?

You experience a payoff whether you achieve your goals or not, and that payoff determines your success. You move toward your dream of becoming a successful writer and author when you receive a positive payoff. For instance, you send out a query letter to an agent because you want to be traditionally published (the positive payoff). You engage readers on social media sites because you know a platform built from many connections will help you land a traditional publishing deal and help your book sell (the positive payoffs).

You choose not to move toward your writing dreams when you're afraid you will receive a negative payoff. For example, you don't send a query letter to an agent to avoid the pain of rejection (the negative payoff). Or you don't finish (or start) your manuscript because you think the process of writing your book will feel difficult or that success will bring unwanted or painful changes in your life (the negative payoffs).

Instead of focusing on potential negative payoffs, train your mind on positive ones. For example, focus on how rewarding it will be to have many people read your work. Or think about the satisfaction or joy you will find in the process of finishing your manuscript and how fabulous your life will be when your career as a writer takes off.

Fearing negative payoffs also blocks you from receiving positive payoffs. The first step in moving past your fear is identification; when you identify your negative payoffs, you become able to focus on the positive ones.

Make a list of your positive and negative payoffs.

My positive payoffs for doing what's necessary to make my dreams real are:	My negative payoffs for not doing what's necessary to make my dreams real are:

Are You a Good Receiver?

If you want to get paid for your work, you must learn how to receive. Your ability to receive is directly proportionate to your ability to earn an income from your writing.

Think about how you accept compliments, testimonials, or even gifts. Are you a good receiver, or do you repel or deflect these offerings with statements like "I don't deserve that," "You shouldn't have," or "That's not true"? Or do you say, "Thank you so much!" "That's awesome!" or "I appreciate that you noticed."

Do you see pennies on the ground and ignore them? Or do you pick them up and thank the universe for bringing you abundance?

Practice receiving gracefully. Receive without any pushback the kind words of others, a smile from a stranger, the money sent to you from readers or customers, an offer of help, or the love of a family member. Just receive.

Describe that experience below, and notice if your ability to receive magnetizes how much you are given.

_____

_____

_____

_____

_____

_____

_____

Are You a Giver?

When you can give so deeply of yourself through your writing—whether a blog post, an article, an essay, or a book—that the monetary transaction doesn't matter to you, you give love to your readers via your work. You share yourself.

Writers who want to make a difference with their work make the most money. They give something valuable to their readers with every piece they publish. According to Tony Robbins, "The common denominator of successful and fulfilled people [is] a hunger to serve something more than yourself."

Stop focusing on what you will get back. Instead, focus on what you can give.

Write something below, and, as you do, focus your intention and your words on giving your readers the most benefit possible. Give of yourself. Don't hold back.

_____

_____

_____

_____

_____

_____

How did it feel to write with this intention? Why?

_____

_____

_____

_____

_____

_____

_____

Publish this work, and notice how it is received.

VISION

"... all things are created twice. There is a mental (first) creation, and a physical (second) creation. The physical follows the mental, just as a building follows a blueprint." **—STEPHEN COVEY**

Can You See Your Destination?

When you see your destination clearly, you know how to reach it. You also develop the confidence that you can navigate to your chosen endpoint.

"Seeing" begins with visualizing your idea or goal. Imagine it in your mind. Create mental pictures of how that state of being or finished product will look and feel. The vision helps you create a map from where you are currently to where you want to go.

In this section's pages, employ your imagination. Add as much detail and engage as many of your senses as you can in your visualizations. Each time you are asked to visualize, answer these questions to help clarify your picture:

- Where am I right now?
- What am I wearing?
- What do I smell?
- What do I feel?
- What do I hear?

Sit up tall, breathe deeply, and allow pictures to fill your mind's eye.

Your visualization ability tends to improve just before sleep and after waking, but you can deliberately daydream at any time. You also can combine your visualizations with affirmations.

Your Definition of Success

To create a vision of success, you first must define what it means to you. Maybe your personal definition of success includes:

- leaving a legacy.
- selling a lot of books.
- making a difference in readers' lives.
- starting a movement.
- changing the world.
- taking readers on a journey.
- giving readers a window into your life or a life they've never lived.
- telling an entertaining or moving story.
- inspiring readers.
- creating a livelihood from your work.

There is no right or wrong definition. Describe or draw your vision of success below.

Success is...

Your Life as a
Successful Author or Writer

You want to become a successful author. Do you know what that life entails?

- How would you spend your days? Why?
- What activities would fill your work time? Why?
- How would this new status or title affect your life?

Answer these questions as you describe your perfect day as a successful author or writer below.

_____

_____

_____

_____

_____

_____

_____

_____

_____

_____

_____

_____

_____

_____

_____

_____

_____

_____

Now spend ten minutes visualizing that life.

Envision Your Book

A publisher once told me, "When I can see a book in my mind's eye, I know the idea is worth pursuing and publishing." Apply this litmus test to your ideas, goals, and dreams. If you can see them, you can make them real.

Take a few moments to visualize your next book, article, essay, or blog post. See it, feel it, experience it!

Now draw it below. Add notations to your drawing to provide extra details. Here are some examples:

- The book has 250 pages.
- The book is a paperback and weighs 1.5 pounds.
- There are ten blurbs on the back cover.
- The cover art accurately portrays the theme.
- This article appeared in [magazine name].
- This magazine has a circulation of 1.5 million.

The book is a hardcover and weighs 3 pounds.

The book has 25 pages.

The cover art acurately portrays the theme.

There are five blurbs on the back cover.

See Yourself as a Successful Author

When you close your eyes and imagine yourself reaching your goal and becoming a successful author or writer, what do you notice?

How do you look?

_____

_____

What's different about your appearance?

_____

_____

Do you behave the same or differently? Why?

_____

_____

How do you speak? Why?

_____

_____

Draw a picture of yourself as a successful author. Use arrows to point out what has changed since you achieved this status.

   Tear out this page and tape it to your bathroom mirror so you see it daily.

The Four Stages of Creation

Create anything, including an idea or a career, by passing it through the following four mystical phases of creation.

- Experience the desire to create something.
- Develop a clear vision of what you plan to create, and focus your thoughts on that vision.
- Feel and believe that you have already created your desire in the physical world.
- Take inspired action to manifest your desire in the physical world.

I know you want to create something! Start the process now.

- **DESIRE:** What is your desire? Don't focus on a specific idea but rather on the urge to bring something new into the world. This desire should align with your passion and purpose. (Example: "I feel the urge to create something that helps shelter animals find forever homes.")
- **THOUGHT:** Conceptualize your desire into a clear thought or idea. What will you create? Can you clearly describe it? (Example: "I want to create a website and blog that provides a guide for adopting pets.")
- **FEELING:** What would it feel like to receive what you desire—to see it physically manifest? Do you feel inspired to take action? What do you feel compelled to do next? (Example: "I feel excited and fulfilled to help shelters, shelter animals, and pet adopters. I want to get my website up immediately and start blogging—and even blog a book! I believe I can do this. I trust in my ability to figure out what to do and how to do it.")
- **ACTION:** What actions are necessary to receive what you desire? (Example: "I have to contact a website designer. I need to plan out my blog and blogged book. I need to connect with shelters for potential partnerships, as well as with pet adopters.")

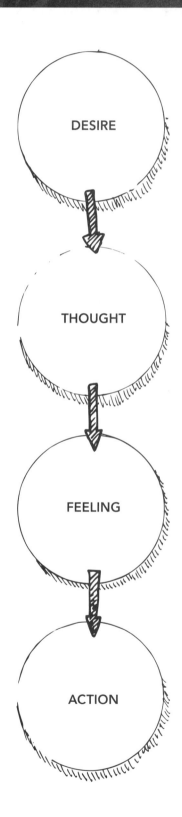

Feel Your Desire

In an instant, the desire to create something new is born within you. At that moment, the transformation from nonphysical to physical begins.

Sit quietly with your eyes closed and your hands on your knees, palms open in a receptive manner. Get in touch with your desire and your inherent ability to create—to make your desires real. If you are a spiritual person, you know you were created in the divine image; therefore, you possess a divine creative ability that allows you to manifest in the world.

What does it feel like to possess this divine desire? Describe the emotions and sensations. At this point, it's not necessary to describe what you want to create, just your desire, your urge to bring something new into the world and, possibly, to have a positive and meaningful impact on others. How does it feel to have the urge to fulfill your potential and purpose?

If it's easier, draw something that depicts your desire to create.

Focus Your Thoughts

From desire, move into the conceptual stage of creation, and begin the process of making your desire a reality.

From a mystical perspective, words have a creative ability. Your thoughts, which consist of words, organize and form matter into physical reality. Once you conceptualize your idea, it begins to materialize.

Among others, Napoleon Hill (*Think and Grow Rich*), Claude M. Bristol (*The Magic of Believing*), James Allen (*As a Man Thinketh*), Wayne Dyer (*Change Your Thoughts, Change Your Life*), and Henriette Klauser (*Write It Down, Make It Happen*) have all taught this lesson. Many people have wit-

nessed firsthand the power of putting their desires into words. For example, Jim Carrey (who wrote a check to himself for $10 million for "services rendered"); Scott Adams, creator of the comic strip Dilbert (who wrote down dreams that came true one by one); and Suze Orman (who affirmed, "I am young, powerful, and successful, producing at least $10,000 per month" every day at the beginning of her career) all saw their thoughts and words made manifest.

Use words to develop clear thoughts of what you want to bring into the world. Use your mind and capacity to think and express to describe what you want to create or write.

I want to create:

_____

_____

Now focus on what you desire. Train your thoughts on your concept—your creation—and only on that. Several times per day, spend at least thirty seconds focused on what you want. To make your thoughts even more powerful, regularly devote longer periods to thinking about and visualizing this!

Connect to Your Feelings

It's now time to enter the formation stage of creation, where you discover the means to make your writing desire real. To do so, combine thought with feeling.

Your emotions serve as guides and motivators. Your inspiration and passion, for instance, drive you to take action to create your desire. Feelings also keep you motivated. When you feel discouraged or stuck, you lack energy and motivation to realize your dreams. When you feel confident and happy, you possess the energy and motivation to take steps toward your goals.

You will know what ideas or actions to pursue based on how the thought of doing so makes you feel. Your feelings work like a GPS, pointing you in the right direction so you know what to do next or where to go to arrive at your destination.

Feelings, like thoughts, possess creative energy. They have an effect in the physical world. (That's why it's so important to feel good!) Align your feelings with what you desire. As Wayne Dyer ex-plained, "The more natural an experience your wish feels for you, the faster you will create it in your life. Conversely, the more unnatural a state of being feels to you, the longer it will take to achieve.

"The key word to contemplate is 'feels.' If being healthy, prosperous, happy, successful, strong, intelligent, and so on currently feel unnatural to you, naturalness may yet be achieved by persistently using your imagination and your subjective attention to make this feeling stick."

Connect your thoughts of what you desire with your feelings of what it will be like to manifest that desire. Take time to imagine having what you want to create—right now. Allow that vision to excite and inspire you and generate other positive feelings.

During your visualization, pay particular attention to any thoughts that pop into your head, or any sense of "inspired action" you receive, that relate to realizing your desire, and write it down.

Take a moment or two to visualize what it would be like if you already had created your idea or career.

Describe how you would behave.

_____

_____

_____

_____

Now, go out and act as if you've already brought your idea into the world or achieved success as a writer.

Create an Action Plan

During the last exercise, did you sense the "inspired action" you need to realize your desire? Did you gain clarity about techniques, tools, or steps you must take to turn your idea into reality? If so, answer these questions:

What actions will you take in the physical world to make your desire a reality? For example, will you send a query letter, finish a book proposal, write daily, or send books to reviewers?

Write your inspired-action steps below.

1. _____
2. _____
3. _____
4. _____
5. _____

Take Inspired Action

The last phase of creation deals with a realm you know well: the physical world. It's time to focus on it, and take action!

In the physical world, you are subject to cause and effect. Turn your desire, which you transformed into thought and feeling in this exercise, into physical action. Use your action plan as a guide.

Now, as Nike says, "Just do it!" Physically effect change as you take the necessary inspired-action steps.

The four stages of creation—desire, thought, feeling, and action—combine into a powerful energy that helps you attract what you desire. In fact, you won't just attract it; you will force your desire into reality using your mind, heart, and body.

Below, track the inspired actions you complete and the results you achieve by doing so. Do your actions bring your ideas and career closer to physical reality?

Inspired Action	Date Completed	Results

Your Gift to Give

Your writing gives a gift to your readers and the world. Imagine the value or benefit inherent in your work. That's the gift you offer.

What gift will you give the world via your work? Envision what is inside the gift box when your readers open it.

Draw your gift below.

Your success hinges on *giving*. However, in the process of giving, you also receive, as do those who purchase your art.

What value or benefit will you *give* your readers?

What will you *receive* in the process of giving your gift to the world?

Visualize "Done"

How do you know when a writing project is complete? Sometimes "done" is a difficult and subjective call. If you know in advance what "done" looks like, you are more likely to attach your work to an e-mail and hit "send."

Don't be a writer who works on a project forever. Instead, visualize "done" by making a list of charac-teristics that qualify your work as complete. Regularly evaluate your work against this list, and then "ship" it out! Release it into the world. Allow your ideas and career to take flight.

Keep Harry S. Truman's words in mind as you complete the exercise below: "Imperfect action beats imperfect inaction every time."

My "done" work includes the following characteristics:

_____

_____

_____

_____

_____

_____

_____

_____

_____

_____

_____

_____

_____

_____

_____

_____

Visualize Your Best-Ever Work

What would it look and feel like to produce your best-ever work?

Your best-ever work could be an e-book that immediately hits the Amazon bestseller list, a blog post that gets a huge amount of engagement (likes and shares), a traditionally published book that starts a movement, or an article that simply feels like the best writing you've ever produced.

Your best-ever work is different from someone else's best-ever work, so only compare your average or regular work to the best work you know you are capable of producing. Don't compare yourself or your work to others.

Close your eyes, and imagine your project and your experience. Then describe them below.

_____

_____

_____

_____

_____

_____

_____

_____

_____

_____

_____

_____

_____

_____

_____

See Yourself Overcoming Obstacles

Athletes visualize themselves achieving success as well as overcoming obstacles, such as physical exhaustion, self-doubt, pain, and competition.

Make a list of the obstacles you might encounter on your way to bringing your idea or dream to life.

For example, you might experience rejection, negative reviews, lack of motivation, too little time, too many other commitments, or fear.

1. _____

2. _____

3. _____

4. _____

5. _____

6. _____

7. _____

8. _____

9. _____

10. _____

Now visualize yourself overcoming each obstacle. You can imagine these obstacles separately or include all of them in one visualization.

Write down how you overcame—jumped over—each obstacle.

Obstacle	Jump

Create a Vision Board

A vision board is a visual representation of what you want to create. It depicts what you want to become and what you want to achieve. The images elicit thoughts of what you want to manifest accompanied by a feeling of having done so.

For example, a picture of an author at a book signing helps you see and feel yourself in that role. It represents you.

Here's an example of a writing- and publishing-focused vision map I crcatcd on a piece of construction paper.

Create your own vision map! Select images from online searches and magazines, and choose any words or phrases you find meaningful. Cut them out, and paste them onto a piece of posterboard. The images can represent a published book, income from your writing, a career as a speaker and writer, or a traditional publishing deal.

Your Ideal Reader

No matter what you write, you must know your intended audience. Visualize your ideal readers so you can write for them!

List ten aspects of your ideal reader.

1. _____
2. _____
3. _____
4. _____
5. _____
6. _____
7. _____
8. _____
9. _____
10. _____

Create an Ideal Reader Profile

You can also get to know your ideal reader by filling out the worksheet below.

MY IDEAL READER PROFILE

AGE: _____

GENDER: _____

PROFESSION: _____

INCOME BRACKET: $0–30,000 $30,001–60,000   60,001–90,000   90,001+

WEBSITES VISITED: _____

OTHER IMPORTANT INFORMATION: _____

_____

_____

Meet Your Ideal Reader

Now mentally "meet" your ideal reader. Draw a picture of this person in the space below, tear out the page, and tape it to your computer so you can keep the reader at the forefront of your intentions as you write.

Commit Your Vision to Words

Your ability to use written words to evoke feelings and images provides a powerful visualization tool. Use that ability now to create a written vision of your most successful year, six months, three months, or month.

Do this yearly to solidify what you want to manifest in the coming twelve months. Do it monthly or quarterly to help you achieve your goals in that time period.

Write your vision in the *present tense*. Use words and phrases that make you feel and see your success as you write about it. Include details about how achieving success as a writer, however you define that, affects other areas of your life.

_____

_____

_____

_____

_____

_____

See Your Vision as a Reality

Now rewrite your *present-tense* vision in the *past tense,* as if it has already happened. For example, imagine the year has ended and you are reviewing your accomplishments. Compose your vision as if the details are no longer ideas, intentions, goals, or desires, but realities. Begin with two sentences like "It's December 31, 2017, and this was my best writing year ever! As a writer, I achieved the following ..."

As you write, feel and see your vision as if it has already become reality.

_____

_____

_____

_____

_____

_____

_____

_____

_____

_____

_____

_____

_____

_____

Tear out this page or photocopy it, and carry it with you. (Or type up your vision, and paste a copy below.) Read your vision before bed and when you wake up each morning.

Visualize Your Best Year Ever

Memorize or record your past-tense vision, and recall or play it back twice a day as you visualize your best year ever.

How do you feel after visualizing your best year? Why?

_____

_____

_____

_____

_____

_____

How would this reality change your career and your life?

_____

_____

_____

_____

_____

_____

_____

_____

What do you now feel inspired to do?

_____

_____

_____

_____

_____

_____

_____

In a Land Far Away and a Time Long Ago

Research suggests that your problem-solving abilities improve when you think about events far in the past or future, or occurring in another location. Imagine yourself as a successful writer in the far-distant future or in a different place. For instance, picture yourself on New Year's Eve twenty years from now, writing a book on some exotic island or speaking to an audience in a foreign country.

If you can't figure out how to overcome a challenge, imagine that you are fifteen years in the future, looking back on the already resolved issue. How did you remove the obstacle in your path?

Write a story below about yourself in the distant future. Begin it this way: *In a land far away and a time long ago …*

_____

_____

_____

_____

_____

_____

_____

_____

_____

_____

_____

_____

_____

_____

_____

_____

_____

Feel Grateful

Sometimes visualizing what you desire, especially as if you already have it, feels difficult. This activity can make you feel inadequate or disheartened because you don't have what you desire … *yet*. You haven't aligned with the feeling of achieving your goals or desires … *yet*.

Develop an attitude of gratitude. This prevents you from suffering in the present moment. While you strive toward what you desire and continue to want it, simply accept where you are. Don't hate your current situation or feel bad about not having reached your destination.

Continue to cultivate a strong desire and will to change your situation for the better. Take action to achieve your writing goals. Until you manifest your desire, you have the ability to *choose* not to suffer.

To do this, learn to be in the moment. Focus on being satisfied with the present. Recognize what you have already created, with gratitude. Feel proud of your accomplishments as you acknowledge that you want to be somewhere else, receive something different, or create something new. Appreciate your current situation.

Start a gratitude journal to help you solidify your new attitude. Every morning and every evening, write down three to five things for which you feel grateful. These can be as small as "I feel grateful for my computer" or as big as "I feel grateful that a literary agent offered me a contract."

Begin your journal by writing three things you feel grateful for right now.

I am grateful for:

1. _____

2. _____

3. _____

GOALS

"A goal properly set is halfway reached." —**ZIG ZIGLAR**

The most successful people in every industry use goals as road maps to help them reach their desired destination. It's no different for writers.

To produce a successful article, essay, book, or career, set goals regularly—and review them often. Make goal setting a daily or weekly activity, not something you only do in December or January. If you didn't meet some of your goals in the last twelve months, then take action to guarantee that this year won't be like the last. If you crushed it over the past twelve months, a repeat performance might be fine. However, you can do, achieve, earn, or produce more this year—or even this month or week. You always can level up.

Follow the lead of high-performing writers, and increase your productivity by developing writing or career goals. Begin by setting the intention for writing success. This first step toward bringing your writing ideas and career to life puts your body in motion toward achieving what you desire.

Clear goals help you arrive at your destination. Remember the Alice Attitude from the Self-Exploration section? If you don't know where you want to end up—and you don't care—you'll arrive *somewhere* but not necessarily at the destination you intended. With an Author Attitude, rather than an Alice Attitude, you choose the direct path to success, and you take it.

The key to acting on your intentions and accomplishing your goals lies in your personal investment in them. You must feel fully committed to achievement in one form or another. Commitment turns your intention into daily action toward achieving goals.

Successful authors report that goals form the foundation of their success. But they don't set goals and forget them like the New Year's resolutions so many of us abandon after the first month. Instead, they review them regularly and evaluate their progress. They break goals into smaller action items and work on that to-do list daily.

As Pablo Picasso said, "Our goals can only be reached through a vehicle of a plan, in which we must fervently believe, and upon which we must vigorously act. There is no other route to success." You can create achievable goals. As you take action on your success plan, you'll find your ideas and career manifesting before your eyes.

Are Your Goals SMART?

How do you set achievable goals? In his classic best-seller *Think and Grow Rich*, Napoleon Hill offers six steps for setting and reaching goals:

1. Have a specific goal.
2. Have a specific time to achieve your goal.
3. Write down your goal.
4. Develop a plan to achieve your goal.
5. Decide what price you are willing to pay.
6. Think about your goal every day.

To make your goals more effective, follow the SMART criteria, commonly attributed to Peter Drucker and George T. Doran:

- **S**pecific: Goals should concisely and clearly define what you plan to do.
- **M**easurable: Goals should be measurable so you have tangible evidence that you have accomplished the goal.
- **A**ttainable: Goals should be achievable yet stretch you slightly so you feel challenged.
- **R**ealistic: Goals must represent an objective toward which you are willing and able to work.
- **T**imebound: Goals should be linked to a time frame that creates a sense of urgency or results in tension between your current reality and your future vision.

It's a smart (excuse the pun) idea to apply SMART goals as you create and review goals for your career.

Choose three writing-related goals you would like to achieve. Apply the SMART characteristics to your goals. Then review these daily or weekly. Here's an example:

GOAL 1: *Begin blogging.*

SPECIFICALLY, I WILL: *write and publish a post twice per week.*

I WILL BE ABLE TO MEASURE WHETHER I HAVE ACHIEVED MY GOAL IN THE FOLLOWING WAYS: *I will have published a blog post twice per week.*

THIS GOAL WILL STRETCH ME IN THE FOLLOWING WAYS: *I will have to learn new technology.*

I KNOW I CAN ATTAIN THIS GOAL BECAUSE: *I am smart and can accomplish anything I set my mind to doing.*

THIS GOAL IS REALISTIC BECAUSE: *It's my purpose to share my message, and accomplishing this goal helps me build the author platform necessary to do so.*

I WILL ACHIEVE THIS GOAL IN THE FOLLOWING TIME FRAME: *by May 15, 2017*

GOAL 1: _____

SPECIFICALLY, I WILL: _____

_____

_____

_____

I WILL BE ABLE TO MEASURE WHETHER I HAVE ACHIEVED MY GOAL IN THE FOLLOWING WAYS: _____

_____

_____

_____

THIS GOAL WILL STRETCH ME IN THE FOLLOWING WAYS: _____

_____

_____

_____

I KNOW I CAN ATTAIN THIS GOAL BECAUSE: _____

_____

_____

_____

THIS GOAL IS REALISTIC BECAUSE: _____

_____

_____

_____

I WILL ACHIEVE THIS GOAL IN THE FOLLOWING TIME FRAME: _____

_____

_____

_____

GOAL 2: _____

SPECIFICALLY, I WILL: _____

_____

_____

_____

I WILL BE ABLE TO MEASURE WHETHER I HAVE ACHIEVED MY GOAL IN THE FOLLOWING WAYS: _____

_____

_____

_____

THIS GOAL WILL STRETCH ME IN THE FOLLOWING WAYS: _____

_____

_____

_____

I KNOW I CAN ATTAIN THIS GOAL BECAUSE: _____

_____

_____

_____

THIS GOAL IS REALISTIC BECAUSE: _____

_____

_____

_____

I WILL ACHIEVE THIS GOAL IN THE FOLLOWING TIME FRAME: _____

_____

_____

_____

GOAL 3: _____

SPECIFICALLY, I WILL: _____

_____

_____

_____

I WILL BE ABLE TO MEASURE WHETHER I HAVE ACHIEVED MY GOAL IN THE FOLLOWING WAYS: _____

_____

_____

_____

THIS GOAL WILL STRETCH ME IN THE FOLLOWING WAYS: _____

_____

_____

_____

I KNOW I CAN ATTAIN THIS GOAL BECAUSE: _____

_____

_____

_____

THIS GOAL IS REALISTIC BECAUSE: _____

_____

_____

_____

I WILL ACHIEVE THIS GOAL IN THE FOLLOWING TIME FRAME: _____

_____

_____

_____

Make Your Goals SMARTER

Now make your goals SMARTER! The SMART goals can prove restrictive, so when you create your writing goals, be sure they also are:

- **S**ensational: Your goals should excite and inspire you. They may be part of a larger goal or a bold, audacious plan.
- **M**oving: You should feel emotionally attached to your goals; they should move you and align with your passion and purpose.
- **A**spirational: Your goals should involve things for which you strive. Taking action toward them should create a sense that you are taking steps to fulfill your purpose and make a meaningful and positive difference in the world or in people's lives.

- **R**elevant: Your goals should have meaning in your life and in relation to the big picture of what you hope to achieve, the legacy you want to leave, how you want to serve others, and the difference you want to make. They should connect to your Big Why.
- **T**imeless: Your goals should be attached to a big picture or vision that extends into the future.
- **E**levating: Your goals should help you level up in some area of your life or career. You should feel as if achieving this goal forces you to be and do better.
- **R**elatable: Your readers, customers, or clients must be able to relate to what your goal produces or helps you achieve. This increases the likelihood they will purchase and read your work.

Define your writing and career goals using SMARTER characteristics. Then read these goals daily or weekly. Here is an example:

GOAL 1: *Publish a book that helps abused women take back their power and create a new life.*

MY GOAL IS SENSATIONAL IN THE FOLLOWING WAYS: *It helps me start a movement to help abused women.*

I FEEL EMOTIONALLY MOVED BY MY GOAL BECAUSE: *It helps me tell my personal abuse story and allows me to support others who share this experience.*

MY GOAL HELPS ME MOVE TOWARD MY ASPIRATIONS IN THE FOLLOWING WAYS: *It helps me become an author and a speaker—someone with the ability to positively affect lives.*

MY GOAL IS RELEVANT TO ME BECAUSE IT RELATES TO MY BIG WHY, WHICH IS: *to empower abused women.*

THIS GOAL IS TIMELESS IN THE FOLLOWING WAYS: *It helps me reach and help abused women not only now but in the future.*

BY ACHIEVING THIS GOAL, I WILL ELEVATE MY LIFE OR CAREER IN THE FOLLOWING WAYS: *I change my status to author and influencer.*

MY READERS, CUSTOMERS, AND CLIENTS WILL RELATE TO THIS PROJECT BECAUSE: *It helps abused women stop feeling powerless so they can take back control of their lives.*

GOAL 1: _____

MY GOAL IS SENSATIONAL IN THE FOLLOWING WAYS: _____

_____

_____

I FEEL EMOTIONALLY MOVED BY MY GOAL BECAUSE: _____

_____

_____

MY GOAL HELPS ME MOVE TOWARD MY ASPIRATIONS IN THE FOLLOWING WAYS: _____

_____

_____

MY GOAL IS RELEVANT TO ME BECAUSE IT RELATES TO MY BIG WHY, WHICH IS: _____

_____

_____

THIS GOAL IS TIMELESS IN THE FOLLOWING WAYS: _____

_____

_____

BY ACHIEVING THIS GOAL, I WILL ELEVATE MY LIFE OR CAREER IN THE FOLLOWING WAYS: _____

_____

_____

MY READERS, CUSTOMERS, AND CLIENTS WILL RELATE TO THIS PROJECT BECAUSE: _____

_____

_____

GOAL 2: _____

MY GOAL IS SENSATIONAL IN THE FOLLOWING WAYS: _____

_____

_____

I FEEL EMOTIONALLY MOVED BY MY GOAL BECAUSE: _____

_____

_____

MY GOAL HELPS ME MOVE TOWARD MY ASPIRATIONS IN THE FOLLOWING WAYS: _____

_____

_____

MY GOAL IS RELEVANT TO ME BECAUSE IT RELATES TO MY BIG WHY, WHICH IS: _____

_____

_____

THIS GOAL IS TIMELESS IN THE FOLLOWING WAYS: _____

_____

_____

BY ACHIEVING THIS GOAL, I WILL ELEVATE MY LIFE OR CAREER IN THE FOLLOWING WAYS: ___

_____

_____

MY READERS, CUSTOMERS, AND CLIENTS WILL RELATE TO THIS PROJECT BECAUSE: _____

_____

_____

GOAL 3: _____

MY GOAL IS SENSATIONAL IN THE FOLLOWING WAYS: _____

_____

_____

I FEEL EMOTIONALLY MOVED BY MY GOAL BECAUSE: _____

_____

_____

MY GOAL HELPS ME MOVE TOWARD MY ASPIRATIONS IN THE FOLLOWING WAYS: _____

_____

_____

MY GOAL IS RELEVANT TO ME BECAUSE IT RELATES TO MY BIG WHY, WHICH IS: _____

_____

_____

THIS GOAL IS TIMELESS IN THE FOLLOWING WAYS: _____

_____

_____

BY ACHIEVING THIS GOAL, I WILL ELEVATE MY LIFE OR CAREER IN THE FOLLOWING WAYS: _____

_____

_____

MY READERS, CUSTOMERS, AND CLIENTS WILL RELATE TO THIS PROJECT BECAUSE: _____

_____

_____

Create Purpose-Driven Goals

Is Your Goal On Purpose?

As you create goals, tie them into your purpose. (See the "What's Your Big Why?" exercise in the Self-Exploration section.) Goals that align with your mission increase your emotional tie and commitment to them. Without this connection, you may never take action to achieve the goal.

If you make purpose-driven decisions about the goals you choose, the tasks you take on, and the opportunities you decide to pursue, you are more likely to remain focused and realize your ideas and career. Therefore, before you do anything—or say yes to anything—answer this question: *Is this on purpose?*

Discern if the goal, task, or opportunity aligns with your greater purpose—the reason you write or want a career as a writer and author. If you take action on a goal, task, or opportunity, doing so should move you closer to fulfilling your purpose.

Below, write down three to five goals, tasks, or opportunities you feel the need to take on. Then evaluate them using the question above: *Is this on purpose?*

Goal, Task, or Opportunity	Is this on purpose?
	☐ Yes ☐ No
	☐ Yes ☐ No
	☐ Yes ☐ No
	☐ Yes ☐ No
	☐ Yes ☐ No

Are You Moving Closer to Your Goal?

Imagine that your writing career is like a car. You want the speedometer to show an increase in speed as you take action toward your goals. You want that needle to move!

Don't put your foot on the gas, though, until you answer this question: *Does this get me closer to my goal?* Similar to the "on-purpose" exercise you worked on previously, this query asks you to evaluate if doing this—whatever "this" is—moves the needle for you.

Will a task, opportunity, or skill, for example, speed up your goal achievement or ability to level up? Will it help you make a quantum leap toward your goal, get you one step closer, keep you where you are, or impede your progress? You don't want to keep traveling at the same speed as before—or worse, drive with the emergency brake on!

List three to five goals, tasks, or opportunities you feel the need to take on. Then evaluate them using this question: *Does this move me closer to my goal?*

Goal, Task, or Opportunity	Does this move me closer to my goal?
	☐ Yes ☐ No
	☐ Yes ☐ No
	☐ Yes ☐ No
	☐ Yes ☐ No
	☐ Yes ☐ No

Do Your Goals, Tasks, and Opportunities Align with Your Values?

Sync your goals, tasks, and opportunities with your values. (Review the values you listed in the "What Do You Value?" exercise in the Self-Exploration section.) Your values are important to you, just like your purpose or mission. When you align your actions and decisions with your values, you become motivated to complete them, and it becomes easier to do so.

Below, evaluate how well the three to five goals, tasks, or opportunities you identified earlier align with your values. To do so, score them on a scale of 1 to 10, with 10 being most aligned and one being least aligned with your values.

GOAL 1: _____ (1 2 3 4 5 6 7 8 9 10)

GOAL 2: _____ (1 2 3 4 5 6 7 8 9 10)

GOAL 3: _____ (1 2 3 4 5 6 7 8 9 10)

GOAL 4: _____ (1 2 3 4 5 6 7 8 9 10)

GOAL 5: _____ (1 2 3 4 5 6 7 8 9 10)

Based on this ranking, which goals and tasks are you more likely to complete?

_____

_____

_____

Is This Part of My Vision?

Picture where you are going and the person you want to become as a writer and author. Then evaluate your goals against this big-picture vision of your career.

To do this, create your vision (see the Vision section of this book), and then determine if you "see" achievement of this goal as part of your future.

Goal	Do you see achievement of this goal as part of your vision for the future?
	☐ Yes ☐ No
	☐ Yes ☐ No
	☐ Yes ☐ No
	☐ Yes ☐ No
	☐ Yes ☐ No

Commit to and work toward smaller goals that help you create your big-picture vision. These will be easy to visualize as achieved, and you clearly will see how they help you reach your overarching goal.

"Should" Versus "Want" Goals

Unfortunately, there are some things you might _need_ to do to become a successful author or writer that you don't _want_ to do. These goals could feel like "have-tos" and "shoulds."

Are you setting some goals because you feel that you _should_ achieve them? If so, ask yourself this question: _Do I_ need _to achieve this goal to bring my idea or career to life, or do I_ want _to achieve it?_

If the answer is that you need to achieve it, change your attitude about the goal. Decide that you _want_ to achieve this goal because it helps you further your writing career.

Evaluate your goals against the Should Versus Want Scale. Then reframe the shoulds into wants. To do so, determine how that smaller goal helps you achieve your overarching goal. Embrace the tasks associated with the smaller goals because they feed your ambition and get results. Here's an example:

GOAL 1: *Publish my book by December 1.*

☑ **SHOULD** ☐ **WANT**

THIS GOAL HELPS ME CREATE MY WRITING DREAM OR CAREER IN THE FOLLOWING WAYS:

1. *It pushes me to finally write my book this year.*

2. *It allows me to start earning income as a writer.*

3. *It allows me to express myself creatively by telling stories.*

GOAL 1: _____

☐ **SHOULD** ☐ **WANT**

THIS GOAL HELPS ME CREATE MY WRITING DREAM OR CAREER IN THE FOLLOWING WAYS:

1. _____

2. _____

3. _____

GOAL 2: _____

☐ **SHOULD** ☐ **WANT**

THIS GOAL HELPS ME CREATE MY WRITING DREAM OR CAREER IN THE FOLLOWING WAYS:

1. _____

2. _____

3. _____

GOAL 3: _____

☐ **SHOULD** ☐ **WANT**

THIS GOAL HELPS ME CREATE MY WRITING DREAM OR CAREER IN THE FOLLOWING WAYS:

1. _____

2. _____

3. _____

Prioritize Your Goals

In our crazy, chaotic, pressure-packed world, you probably juggle multiple priorities every day. The same may be true in your writing career. In any given moment, however, one of those priorities has to become your *only priority.*

You only can focus on one goal at a time, and doing so helps you achieve it. Maybe the deadline for an article assignment is fast approaching; that job becomes Priority Number 1 until you have achieved it.

That doesn't mean you don't take action toward other goals but that you spend the majority of your time completing the steps that allow you to finish your top-priority assignment.

Place your top-priority goal on the front burner, and turn up the heat. At the same time, move other goals to the back burners, where you can keep an eye on them. Allow them to simmer until you are ready to move them forward.

Prioritize the three goals you previously defined using the SMART and SMARTER characteristics. Which one do you want or have to accomplish first? That's Priority Number 1. Which must come second and third?

My Goal Achievement Priority List

PRIORITY NUMBER 1: _____

PRIORITY NUMBER 2: _____

PRIORITY NUMBER 3: _____

If you have other goals you'd like to achieve, you can add them to the list as well. Then start working toward achieving them, one action step at a time. (Learn more about how to do this in the next exercise.)

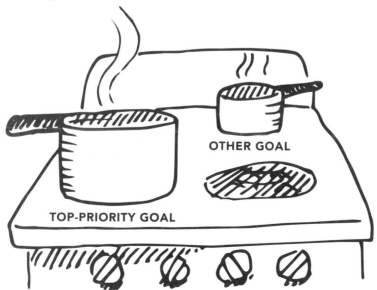

Short-Term and Long-Term Goals

Break down your goals into two types: short-term and long-term.

Short-term goals are those you want to accomplish in the next day, week, or few months. For example, maybe you want to finish a blog post or essay, send out query letters to agents, or get your website up and running. Tasks such as getting a logo designed, arranging headshots, or conducting an interview fall into the short-term goal category, too.

Long-term goals are those you want to accomplish this year, next year, or even further into the future because they take longer to achieve. For example, releasing a traditionally published book can take more than a year. Completing a novel might take you more than twelve months if you count revisions and working with an editor. Developing a strong author platform also might be a long-term goal.

Work on both types of goals. As you do, "chunk down" the goal and create a smaller task list to help you make consistent progress.

Short-Term Goals

First, focus on your short-term goals. Look at your list of goals from the previous exercise. Can you complete any of them in a short amount of time? If so, add them below. If not, brainstorm for a moment and think about three to five things you need to accomplish today, this week, or this month. These might be smaller tasks related to your long-term goals.

Next, think of each goal like a huge rock you need to move. If you could use a sledgehammer to break off chunks of the rock (goals) so you ended up with smaller, more easily moved pieces, what would they be? Think of these chunks as small tasks or action items to include on your daily to-do list. Add them to the related goal below. Here's an example:

SHORT-TERM GOAL 1: *Get a professional headshot.*

ACTION ITEMS:

1. *Research photographers.*
2. *Set up an appointment.*
3. *Purchase an outfit for the shoot.*
4. *Do the photoshoot.*
5. *Choose the best photo.*

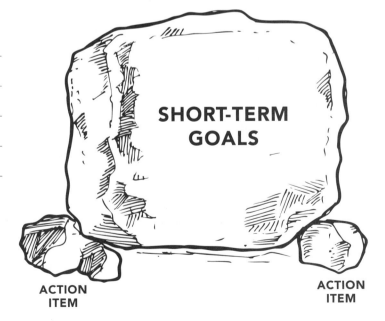

SHORT-TERM GOALS

ACTION ITEM

ACTION ITEM

SHORT-TERM GOAL 1: _____

ACTION ITEMS:

1. _____

2. _____

3. _____

4. _____

5. _____

SHORT-TERM GOAL 2: _____

ACTION ITEMS:

1. _____

2. _____

3. _____

4. _____

5. _____

SHORT-TERM GOAL 3: _____

ACTION ITEMS:

1. _____

2. _____

3. _____

4. _____

5. _____

SHORT-TERM GOAL 4: _____

ACTION ITEMS:

1. _____

2. _____

3. _____

4. _____

5. _____

SHORT-TERM GOAL 5: _____

ACTION ITEMS:

1. _____

2. _____

3. _____

4. _____

5. _____

Now add these tasks to your calendar, and enjoy the satisfaction as you move quickly and efficiently toward your goals, marking each action item as done.

Long-Term Goals

Break down your long-term goals into manageable pieces using the same process.

List your long-term goals, and chunk them down into action items you can complete on a daily or weekly basis as you move toward goal achievement. Here's an example:

LONG-TERM GOAL 1: _Self-publish my novel by November 30, 2017._

ACTION ITEMS:

1. _Write daily, and complete the first draft by August 1._

2. _Find and work with a developmental editor; complete this process by September 1._

3. _Find and work with a line editor; complete this process by October 1._

4. _Get a cover designed by October 1._

5. _Get the book interior formatted by November 1._

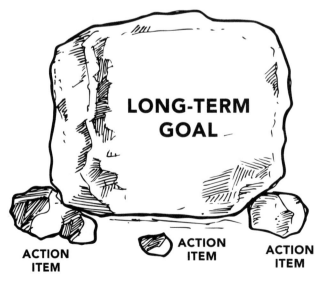

ACTION ITEM   ACTION ITEM   ACTION ITEM

LONG-TERM GOAL 1: _____

ACTION ITEMS:

1. _____

2. _____

3. _____

4. _____

5. _____

LONG-TERM GOAL 2: _____

ACTION ITEMS:

1. _____

2. _____

3. _____

4. _____

5. _____

LONG-TERM GOAL 3: _____

ACTION ITEMS:

1. _____

2. _____

3. _____

4. _____

5. _____

LONG-TERM GOAL 4: _____

ACTION ITEMS:

1. _____

2. _____

3. _____

4. _____

5. _____

LONG-TERM GOAL 5: _____

ACTION ITEMS:

1. _____

2. _____

3. _____

4. _____

5. _____

Add these tasks to your calendar, and mark them as done as you complete them.

Create Clear Publishing Goals

It's one thing to say you want to turn your idea into a book, article, essay, or blog. It's quite another to have a clear, written goal that contributes to your larger goal of becoming an author or writer.

You must know what it means to "become an author" or "have a career as a writer." What will it take to achieve that long-term goal, and how will you know when you've done so?

Take the time to journal about your goal of becoming an author. Use the SMART and SMARTER goals in this section. Be certain your publishing goal aligns with your purpose, values, and vision. (See the Self-Evaluation section for more on these topics.)

It's possible that you identified your long-term goal in an earlier exercise. You might want to traditionally publish or self-publish a book, for example. Many people choose to work on short-term goals, such as "Write a chapter in my book," rather than long-term ones like "Become an author." But you need clarity on your big goals, too.

MY BIG LONG-TERM PUBLISHING GOAL: _____

SPECIFICALLY, I WILL: _____

_____

_____

_____

I WILL BE ABLE TO MEASURE WHETHER I HAVE ACHIEVED MY GOAL IN THE FOLLOWING WAYS: _____

_____

_____

_____

THIS GOAL WILL STRETCH ME IN THE FOLLOWING WAYS: _____

_____

_____

_____

I KNOW I CAN ATTAIN THIS GOAL BECAUSE: _____

_____

_____

_____

THIS GOAL IS REALISTIC BECAUSE: _____

_____

_____

_____

I WILL ACHIEVE THIS GOAL IN THE FOLLOWING TIME FRAME: _____

_____

_____

_____

MY GOAL IS SENSATIONAL IN THE FOLLOWING WAYS: _____

_____

_____

_____

I FEEL EMOTIONALLY MOVED BY MY GOALS BECAUSE: _____

_____

_____

_____

MY GOAL HELPS ME MOVE TOWARD MY ASPIRATIONS IN THE FOLLOWING WAYS: _____

_____

_____

_____

MY GOAL IS RELEVANT TO ME BECAUSE IT RELATES TO MY BIG WHY, WHICH IS: _____

_____

_____

_____

THIS GOAL IS TIMELESS IN THE FOLLOWING WAYS: _____

_____

_____

_____

BY ACHIEVING THIS GOAL, I WILL ELEVATE MY LIFE OR CAREER IN THE FOLLOWING WAYS: _____

_____

_____

_____

MY READERS, CUSTOMERS, AND CLIENTS WILL RELATE TO THIS PROJECT BECAUSE: _____

_____

_____

_____

Evaluate how your goal aligns with your values, using a scale of 1 to 10, where 10 is most aligned and 1 is least aligned.

1   2   3   4   5   6   7   8   9   10

Is this goal on purpose?

☐ YES   ☐ NO

Article Sales Goals

You need both short-term and long-term goals to write and publish essays and articles. The short-term goals relate to getting assignments, finishing jobs, getting your work published, and getting paid. Your long-term goals relate to getting more assignments or having enough income from your work to create a true livelihood.

As you draft your goals, think about these questions: Why are you writing these pieces? For example, do you want to get paid as a writer, create your platform, or promote your books? The reason you write essays and articles affects your long-term goal of creating a professional writing career.

Use the space below to journal about your overarching goal of becoming a professional writer, journalist, or essayist. Use the SMART and SMARTER goals in this section. Be certain these goals align with your purpose, values, and vision.

_____

_____

_____

_____

_____

It's possible that these goals are on a list you created previously. If so, take a big-picture look at what you want to accomplish. Be certain you have a goal that speaks to your desire to publish your work and achieve a long-term goal.

Think big! How do these articles brand you? Can they be turned into books? Is there a way to attach these goals to a more audacious goal?

MY BIG PROFESSIONAL WRITING GOAL:_____

_____

_____

_____

SPECIFICALLY, I WILL: _____

_____

_____

_____

I WILL BE ABLE TO MEASURE WHETHER I HAVE ACHIEVED MY GOAL IN THE FOLLOWING WAYS: _____

_____

_____

_____

THIS GOAL WILL STRETCH ME IN THE FOLLOWING WAYS: _____

_____

_____

_____

I KNOW I CAN ATTAIN THIS GOAL BECAUSE: _____

_____

_____

_____

THIS GOAL IS REALISTIC BECAUSE: _____

_____

_____

_____

I WILL ACHIEVE THIS GOAL IN THE FOLLOWING TIME FRAME: _____

_____

_____

_____

MY GOAL IS SENSATIONAL IN THE FOLLOWING WAYS: _____ _____

_____

_____

_____

I FEEL EMOTIONALLY MOVED BY MY GOALS BECAUSE: _____

_____

_____

_____

MY GOAL HELPS ME MOVE TOWARD MY ASPIRATIONS IN THE FOLLOWING WAYS: _____

_____

_____

_____

MY GOAL IS RELEVANT TO ME BECAUSE IT RELATES TO MY BIG WHY, WHICH IS: _____

_____

_____

_____

THIS GOAL IS TIMELESS IN THE FOLLOWING WAYS: _____

_____

_____

_____

BY ACHIEVING THIS GOAL, I WILL ELEVATE MY LIFE OR CAREER IN THE FOLLOWING WAYS: _____

_____

_____

_____

MY READERS, CUSTOMERS, AND CLIENTS WILL RELATE TO THIS PROJECT BECAUSE: _____

_____

_____

_____

Evaluate how your goal aligns with your values, using a scale of 1 to 10, where 10 is most aligned, and 1 is least aligned.

1	2	3	4	5	6	7	8	9	10

Is this goal on purpose?

☐ **YES**   ☐ **NO**

Book Sales Goals

If you want to write and publish books, it's enormously important to have specific goals related to book sales. If you want to sell enough copies to become a *New York Times* or Amazon best-selling author, you need to know what that takes and create goals that can make that dream real.

Or maybe becoming a best-selling author doesn't interest you. You want your book to make a differ-

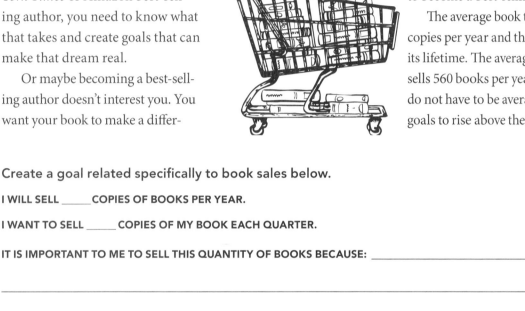

ence in a few people's lives, leave a legacy for your kids, or boost your business. In these cases, the number of copies you want to sell—or give away— differs from that of someone who wants to become a best-selling author.

The average book today only sells 250 copies per year and three thousand in its lifetime. The average e-book author sells 560 books per year. You, of course, do not have to be average! Set book sales goals to rise above the competition.

Create a goal related specifically to book sales below.

I WILL SELL _____ **COPIES OF BOOKS PER YEAR.**

I WANT TO SELL _____ **COPIES OF MY BOOK EACH QUARTER.**

IT IS IMPORTANT TO ME TO SELL THIS QUANTITY OF BOOKS BECAUSE: _____

_____

_____

_____

Now journal about why you want to sell that many books. What's your reason?

_____

_____

_____

Are you committed to doing what it takes to reach that goal? Why?

_____

_____

Twenty Ways to Promote Your Book

To achieve your book sales goal, develop a book promotion or marketing plan. This consists of ways in which you will help sell your book or get it in the hands of readers.

Brainstorm all the possible ways you can reach potential readers and tell them about your book. Think outside the box. Consider where your readers hang out, both online and off. Be creative!

TWENTY WAYS I WILL PROMOTE MY BOOK

1. _____

2. _____

3. _____

4. _____

5. _____

6. _____

7. _____

8. _____

9. _____

10. _____

11. _____

12. _____

13. _____

14. _____

15. _____

16. _____

17. _____

18. _____

19. _____

20. _____

Here are a few examples:

1. Speak at conferences in my target market.
2. Write articles for publications in my target market.
3. Create a course that elaborates on the topic of my book.
4. Send e-mails to my mailing list to tell potential readers the book is now available.
5. Create and publish press releases.
6. Arrange a virtual or blog tour.
7. Seek out reviewers.

Your Raving Fan Base

The work you devote to spreading the word before your book's release is almost as important as the effort you put in afterward. To ensure your book promotion efforts work, create an author platform. You need this foundation of raving fans that can't wait to purchase your book once it is published. They are people to whom you promote your book upon publication. Once you have an author platform, you can promote your book both before and after release.

Create a platform by writing for publications, blogging, getting involved in social networks, producing and sharing YouTube videos, podcasting, appearing on radio and television shows, creating an e-mail list, and speaking at live events. Anything you do that gives you visibility, reach, authority, and influence in your target market builds your author platform.

Start thinking about an author platform when you first get the idea for a book. A platform isn't built in a day, a week, a month, or even a year. It takes considerable time and effort.

Below, make a list of activities that will help you build a platform and promote your book prior to release. For each one, create three action items to accomplish that task. Here is an example:

PLATFORM-BUILDING ACTIVITY: *Create a mailing list of potential readers and buyers.*

ACTION STEPS:

1. *Develop a free product to offer potential readers or buyers in exchange for their e-mail address.*

2. *Post this offer on my website.*

3. *Create a landing page for this offer, and promote it on social networks.*

PLATFORM-BUILDING ACTIVITY: _____

ACTION STEPS:

1. _____

2. _____

3. _____

PLATFORM-BUILDING ACTIVITY: _____

ACTION STEPS:

1. _____

2. _____

3. _____

PLATFORM-BUILDING ACTIVITY: _____

ACTION STEPS:

1. _____

2. _____

3. _____

PLATFORM-BUILDING ACTIVITY: _____

ACTION STEPS:

1. _____

2. _____

3. _____

PLATFORM-BUILDING ACTIVITY: _____

ACTION STEPS:

1. _____

2. _____

3. _____

PLATFORM-BUILDING ACTIVITY: _____

ACTION STEPS:

1. _____

2. _____

3. _____

PLATFORM-BUILDING ACTIVITY: _____

ACTION STEPS:

1. _____

2. _____

3. _____

What's Your Book About?

As an author, you have many opportunities to tell people about your book. However, when they ask, "What's your book about?" that's not what they want to know. They really mean, "What's in it for me?" So answer that question instead.

Potential readers are interested in the value your book may provide. Both fiction and nonfiction offer benefits. Locate this information on the back cover or jacket flap of most books.

Even before your book is published, you can prepare this marketing information in the form of a *pitch*. Also known as an "elevator speech," a pitch is a brief description of your book's central idea, story, or theme. For a novel, it stresses the pivotal incident that changes a character or with which the character struggles. For nonfiction, the pitch focuses on the book's benefit, the target market, and on what makes it unique and necessary within a particular bookstore category. You can pitch your book idea to agents, acquisitions editors, and potential readers.

Here's the pitch I wrote for this book:

> *Creative Visualization for Writers: An Interactive Guide for Bringing Your Ideas and Career to Life* will help writers utilize both sides of the brain to become more creative, confident, and productive ideators. Part adult coloring book, part creative journal, diary, and workbook, and part self-help guide, *Creative Visualization for Writers* will be SARK's *Make Your Creative Dreams Real* meets Shakti Gawain's *Creative Visualization* or Rhonda Byrne's *The Secret*. It will take advantage of the hot adult coloring book trend while providing the substance necessary to sustain sales over time.

When my agent, Gordon Warnock of Fuse Literary, announced the deal in *Publishers Weekly*, it read this way:

> Nina Amir's *CREATIVE VISUALIZATION FOR WRITERS: An Interactive Guide for Bringing Your Ideas and Career to Life*, is *Wreck This Journal* for authors and features 150 unconventional exercises to bridge the gap from idea to book.

A pitch for fiction might look like this one from artist, composer, writer, and podcaster Alex White:

> *Every Mountain Made Low* by Alex White is a taut thriller with paranormal elements set in a dystopian, subterranean Birmingham, Alabama. This is a standalone novel with series potential.
>
> Life is cruel in the Hole, and so is death. All the women in Loxley's family have had the ability to see the restless dead, but ghosts see Loxley back. They're drawn to her like a bright fire, and their lightest touch leaves her with painful wounds. She avoids them as best she can—but she can't say no to the specter of Nora, her only friend, who was alive just hours ago. Loxley is autistic and suffers from crippling anxiety; she isn't equipped to solve a murder, but if she can't bring Nora's killers to justice then no one ever will.
>
> Loxley swears to take blood for blood and find her friend's killer. In the process, she uncovers a conspiracy that rises all the way to the top of the Hole. As her enemies grow wise to her existence, she becomes the quarry, hunted by a brutal enforcer of the corporate interests who rule the city. Hunted and alone in the world, Loxley must descend into the strangest depths of the Hole to win the revenge she seeks and, ultimately, her own salvation.

For more information on writing a pitch, refer to my book *The Author Training Manual*.

Craft your pitch below:

_____

_____

_____

_____

_____

_____

I'm an Author! Now What?

Your book has been published. WOOT! Now what?

This is a big achievement. You have a new title: *Author*. You have a book in your hand to prove you have accomplished your goal.

You need to celebrate! How will you do that? Will you host a book release party, go out to dinner with your family and friends, or take a day off to sit on the beach and relax?

Draw a picture below of how you plan to acknowledge your achievement.

Also, journal about how you feel right now!

_____

_____

_____

_____

_____

_____

Put Your Book in Readers' Hands

Now that your book is published, make it available! Draft a list of all the people to whom you will send your book. These can be family and friends or reviewers and contributors. You want to be sure to share your good news!

And don't forget to follow through on your promotion plan.

I will send my new book to the following people:

1. _____

2. _____

3. _____

4. _____

5. _____

6. _____

7. _____

8. _____

9. _____

10. _____

Draw a Map to Success

Your goals constitute a map that leads from where you are now to where you want to go (the destination you defined in the Vision section). Do you know how to get there or what stops you need to make along the way?

Map out the path from your current location to your final destination. Be sure to include your estimated time of arrival (ETA) for each stop and any-thing you have to do to ensure that you arrive on schedule.

Fill in the map below, noting your current location and your intended destination. Draw an *X* on the path to indicate a stop you must make on your way to your destination. Include where you are now, where you want to go with your work or career, and the stops or places you must visit along the way.

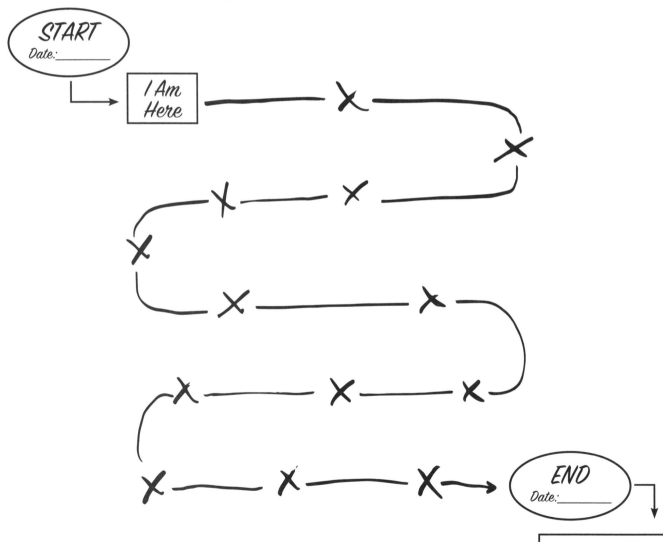

Embrace Work

The publishing world is replete with opportunities to become a writer and author, and to develop a lucrative career doing what you love—putting words on paper. As best-selling author Brendon Burchard says, "When you knock on the door of opportunity, it is work who answers."

It's time to look work in the eye and embrace it. Maybe your work entails one or more of the following:

- **WRITING YOUR MANUSCRIPT:** making time daily to produce a certain number of pages or words
- **BUILDING YOUR AUTHOR PLATFORM:** blogging several times per week, getting involved in social networks, speaking, producing YouTube videos, podcasting, etc.
- **PROMOTING YOUR EXISTING BOOKS:** creating visuals to share on social networks, guest blogging, appearing on podcasts and radio shows, writing articles, etc.
- **CREATING A WEBSITE:** working with a designer or doing it yourself

When you accept the opportunity and walk through the door, what will your work look like? Draw a picture below.

You Can Do It!

Sometimes your goals, while inspirational and exciting, feel overwhelming. They bring up your fears and self-doubts. They make you uncomfortable.

At those times, remind yourself of one important fact: *You can do it!*

Color in these statements.

Really, you can. You've got this. Close your eyes, and say the following words ten times with conviction. (If you're alone, feel free to shout!)

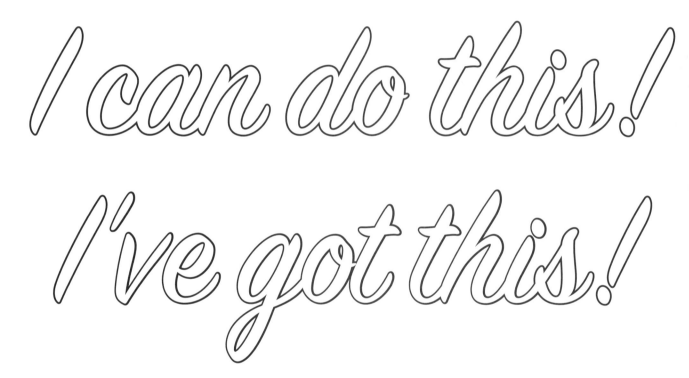

Now take a deep breath or two. Sit down at your computer. Tackle your to-do list. Get at least one thing done that moves you toward your goal.

In the process, you'll realize that, indeed, you can do this and you've got what it takes to succeed.

Stay on Purpose!

Stay on purpose! It's easy to find yourself chasing the next shiny object and ending up doing a ton of things that have no connection to your goals. If you find yourself feeling lost, overwhelmed, or unsure about why you are doing what you're doing, reconnect with your purpose. (See the "What's Your Big Why?" exercise in the Self-Exploration section.)

Are you on purpose today? How?

_____

_____

_____

_____

_____

Are all your goals, actions, and opportunities on purpose?

_____

_____

_____

_____

_____

Or are you chasing some shiny object down a roundabout path? What is the object, and why are you running after it?

_____

_____

_____

_____

_____

_____

Go for It!

When you procrastinate or feel anxious about taking action toward your goals, remember what best-selling author Tony Robbins says: "Stop being afraid of what could go wrong, and start being excited about what could go right."

Go for it! Use these queries to move toward your goals right now.

What will you go for today?

_____

_____

_____

_____

This week?

_____

_____

_____

_____

This month?

_____

_____

_____

_____

Now go do something that moves you toward your goal!

Go for it!

Acknowledge Your Achievements

After you work long and hard to achieve a goal, it's extremely common to simply turn to the next one on your list. If you don't stop to allow your accomplishments to sink in, you may feel as if you never make progress at all.

Acknowledge your accomplishments. Celebrate them before you move on to the next task at hand. Give yourself credit for your achievements.

Celebrate big and small undertakings. For example, you can acknowledge getting everything done on your to-do list today; doing something daring, like contacting ten agents or sending a query to a magazine editor; finishing the first draft of your manuscript; or landing a traditional book deal.

Whatever goal you achieve, celebrate it! And celebrate *you*!

Celebrate!

Plan your goal-achievement celebration below. Draw a picture of how you will celebrate. If you want, also journal about what you will do to acknowledge and enjoy your achievements. For instance, you can plan a personal retreat, a party, or a trip to your favorite ice-cream parlor.

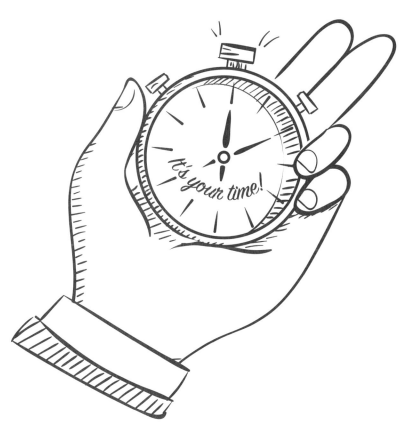

CREATIVITY

"Creativity is a habit, and the best creativity is the result of good work habits." —**TWYLA THARP**

Can You Create at Will?

You sit down at the computer each day, put your fingers on the keyboard, and pause. *Shazam!* Inspiration hits, and your fingers begin to move across the keys faster than you thought possible. Words, sentences, and paragraphs form on the screen in front of you. Several hours later you emerge from the "zone," take a deep breath, and leave your work for the day.

Is that how you imagine the writer's life?

In reality, many writers struggle to get the first word, sentence, or page written. They force themselves to stay at their desks for hours, all the while hoping to produce at least one or two usable manuscript pages.

And sometimes they can't write or produce anything usable. You've seen funny illustrations of someone with writer's block: head in hands and waste bin overflowing with crumpled attempts.

Here's the thing. Your writing life could be as you imagined—filled with creativity and productivity. It's possible. Really, it is.

You just need to know how to turn on your creativity at will.

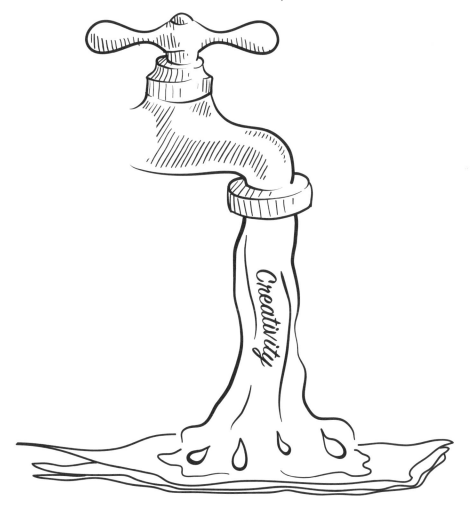

Is Your Well Empty or Full?

Creativity is like a well: Sometimes it's empty, and other times it's full. However, you can ensure your creativity well overflows with a constant stream of ideas.

To do so, draw from your other wells: your sources of energy, ideas, clarity, courage, love, excitement, joy, relationships, education, and productivity. These all affect the contents of your creativity well. Below, determine each well's current water level.

On a scale of 1 to 10, with 10 being full capacity, how empty or full are your wells: energy, ideas, clarity, courage, love, excitement, joy, relationships, education, and productivity? (Photocopy this page and shade in the water level in the illustration for each of your wells.)

Why?

_____

_____

_____

_____

_____

_____

_____

How can you fill each well?

_____

_____

_____

_____

_____

_____

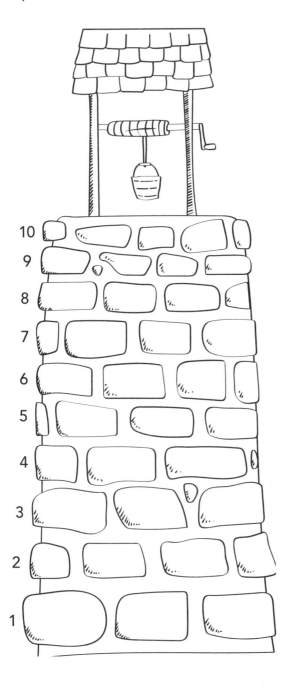

Create a Sacred Writing Space

Creativity must be coaxed out to become habitual. Spiritual traditions offer a great model for this behavior, because they provide a sacred space in which to conduct rituals regularly. This creates a vortex of spiritual energy in that space. You need only enter the sanctuary to strengthen and enrich your connection with the Divine Spirit.

In the same manner, create a vortex of creative energy in your workspace by making it sacred. Elevate your work from ordinary to extraordinary. Allow yourself to connect to your higher self, a higher power, or your soul's purpose as you write. Doing so increases your creativity and flow, and gives your writing the reverence it deserves.

Consistently use this space to write and connect with your muse, and over time your creativity will kick in—or your muse will show up—every time you enter the space. Eventually your mind will connect being creative with the habit of sitting down at your desk.

To create a sacred writing space, place in your work area anything that inspires you, including mementos, candles, objects related to hobbies, vision boards, journals, and incense. Bring in spiritual objects as well, such as a photo of a saint or guru, crystals, or religious symbols.

Draw your sacred writing or creativity space below. You also can create a list of objects you want to include. Then go create it!

Your Creativity Ritual

Many athletes and actors complete rituals prior to performing. They might put on a special pair of socks, say a prayer, or do a stretching routine. This gets them in the zone and helps them feel comfortable and confident. You can approach writing similarly.

Develop a creativity (or writing) ritual. It can be similar to a religious or spiritual ritual. For instance, as part of your sacred office space, create an altar. Every day before you sit down to write, go to your altar and light candles and incense, say a prayer or recite an inspiring mantra, and then sit down at your desk.

Writing rituals help you get in the flow. They form an environment or energetic space that helps you focus, access your muse, and feel creative.

Rituals serve as triggers. Writing rituals remind your mind and body it's time to write. Triggers help you start writing faster and complete more work. They launch you into a flow state.

Your ritual can be as simple as listening to calming music, meditating for five minutes, or jotting down a brief intention for your writing period. It can be as elaborate as doing a sacred dance or walking ten times around your desk to limber up before you put fingers to keyboard. Maybe you wear the same sweatshirt during each writing session or recite a specific affirmation.

Design a creativity ritual for yourself—something that helps you connect with your muse or tap into the flow of ideas and words. Describe what you will do, step by step, below.

_____

_____

_____

_____

_____

_____

_____

_____

_____

Practice Creativity

Do you have a spiritual, yoga, or meditation practice? Maybe you play a sport and attend soccer, swim, or basketball practices. You also need a creativity practice to help you hone that skill and readily access your creative ability.

For example, every morning prior to writing, you might complete some "creativity warmups," like a quick mind-mapping or journaling exercise. Maybe you set an alarm and write for fifteen minutes without pause about whatever comes to mind.

Maybe your creativity practice is *writing*—putting words on paper. You go into your office, sit down, and turn on your creativity by writing for an hour or two every day.

What will your creativity practice look like or involve? Describe it below—and then schedule your practice periods.

_____

_____

_____

_____

_____

_____

_____

_____

_____

_____

_____

_____

_____

_____

_____

_____

_____

Energize Your Creativity

According to William Shatner, "Energy is the key to creativity." Indeed, your energy level affects your ability to succeed as a writer. Without energy, you struggle to work. With energy, you can work for lengthy periods.

What gives you energy? For example, getting eight hours of sleep, cutting out gluten, meditating, or exercising might give you a much-needed boost.

And what gives your writing energy? Reading, attending a class, getting outside in nature, or meeting with other writers all affect and influence your words.

Make two lists below, one with things that energize you and one with things that energize your writing. Then incorporate these energizing activities into your daily or weekly creativity routine.

The following things energize me:

1. _____
2. _____
3. _____
4. _____
5. _____
6. _____
7. _____
8. _____
9. _____
10. _____

The following things energize my writing:

1. _____
2. _____
3. _____
4. _____
5. _____
6. _____
7. _____
8. _____
9. _____
10. _____

Become a Creative Energizer Bunny

Model the Energizer Bunny: Keep creating and writing long after other writers have lost the ability or desire to produce work. To do so, you need heightened and sustained levels of energy.

Create a list of ways to increase both your personal energy and the energy you devote to your creativity and writing. For example, you could try these simple methods:

- Sleep more.
- Improve your diet.
- Drink more water.
- Get out into nature daily.
- Take frequent breaks.
- Exercise three times per week.
- Walk daily.

Ten things I could do to increase my energy, creativity, and productivity:

1. _____
2. _____
3. _____
4. _____
5. _____
6. _____
7. _____
8. _____
9. _____
10. _____

Now energize your body and your mind for writing.

Mind Map Any Idea or Project

Have you ever gotten an idea and not known how to bring it to life? Or do you need a big-picture view of everything that a project comprises but have a myopic view of the idea? You might feel like you can't organize the information or that your idea feels too big, too unwieldy, too confusing. Or it might feel too small; you can't build it out.

Solve these problems with a mind map. This visual-thinking tool explores ideas and concepts graphically and helps you switch from left-brain thinking to right-brain thinking, structure information, and analyze, comprehend, synthesize, recall, and generate new ideas.

Mind mapping uses the power of free association or brainstorming around a concept. That concept lives at the center of a blank page. You then add words, images, or phrases around the central concept. Each lives in its own circle and is connected by lines.

You can use apps or programs to mind map if you like. You also can use a large piece of posterboard and some colored pens or sticky notes, or a whiteboard.

Allow your mind to connect one idea to the next. Let your ideas flow like an electric current, each one lighting up in succession. Then organize the ideas by connecting them with lines and circles or by moving the sticky notes around into clusters of related topics. In this way, you can control the current. Force it to flow in a more logical and useful manner.

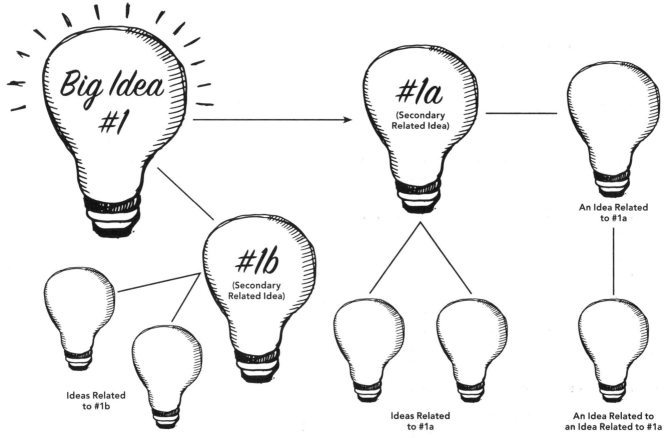

Big Idea #1

#1a
(Secondary Related Idea)

An Idea Related to #1a

#1b
(Secondary Related Idea)

Ideas Related to #1b

Ideas Related to #1a

An Idea Related to an Idea Related to #1a

Dump Your Ideas

Use a mind map to dump your ideas onto the page. Pick a writing project, and dump all your related ideas—and your thoughts—below.

Brain Dump!

From there, you can clean up the brain dump by organizing your ideas and thoughts into a mind map. (See later exercises in this section.)

Create a Brainstorm

Mind maps help you brainstorm. The process activates your brain and your big idea to trigger a downpour of related ideas. Every once in a while, a bolt of lightning shoots through your mind—another great idea generated to bring the original idea to life.

Create a brainstorm for an idea below.

Switch on Your Light Bulbs

Sit in a dark room. Give your eyes and mind a break from all the distractions. Daydream. Meditate. Nap.

Then open your eyes, and allow your mind to play with ideas … or your need for an idea. Wait for the light bulb to turn on.

Write down your light bulb moments below. Don't filter out the ones you perceive as "bad." Just jot them all down.

Can you connect any of the light bulbs? If so, draw a line between them.

Mind Map a Book Concept

Below, create a mind map of a book idea. When finished, use the map to help you write a detailed table of contents.

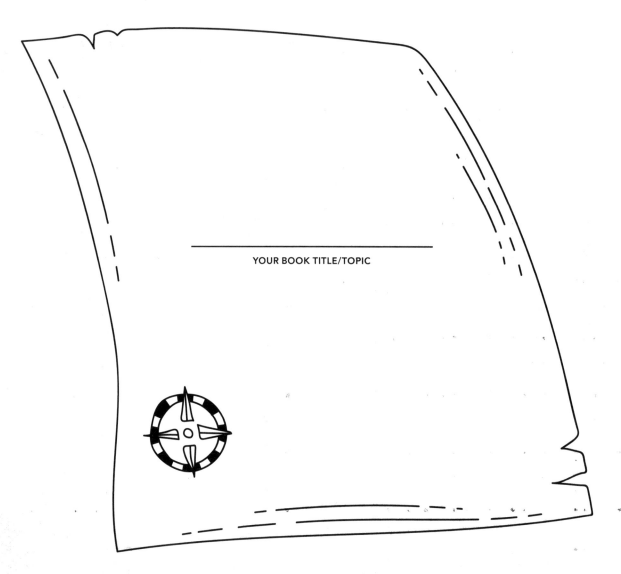

YOUR BOOK TITLE/TOPIC

TABLE OF CONTENTS

Mind Map an Article Concept

Do you have an idea for an article or essay? Super! Use a mind map to figure out how to start, what content will appear in the middle, and how you will end the piece.

Mind map your essay or article below.

Mind Map a Course or Talk Related to Your Book

Here's a great way to promote a book, build a platform around a book, develop expert status, or earn some extra income: Produce courses and speeches, training sessions, webinars, or teleseminars based on your work. If you aren't sure how to get started, try a mind map!

Pick a topic about which you would like to speak. (It should relate in some way to your writing.) This could be a chapter in your nonfiction book, a theme that runs through all your novels, or a "signature story" that relates to how you became published.

Next, use a mind map to brainstorm all the possible information about which you could speak or on which you could train.

For example, if you wrote a book about how to achieve goals, you might want to produce a talk or series of webinars on this topic. (You could then turn this talk or series into a course—see my e-book, *Authorpreneur*, for more information on how to do this.) You might create a first video about why goals are important. The second video could discuss how to set goals. The third could be about how to achieve goals. Before recording each video, mind map the information you would cover. For example, for the second video, you might talk about SMART goals, emotional tie-in, or purpose.

Mind map a course, teleseminar, webinar, or speech below.

Mind Map Products and Services

You can provide products and services to your fans and followers, such as courses, T-shirts, a podcast, speaking, or coaching.

Below, mind map product and service possibilities. Keep your themes, topics, and expertise in mind as you do so.

Don't forget to mind map what you have to do to make these monetization methods a reality. That means you must create a to-do list for each idea.

Here's an example of a to-do list you might put together from a mind map.

Book $\rightarrow$ · Online course
· Speeches
· Consulting

Online Course $\rightarrow$ **To Do**
· Create curriculum
· Record videos
· Develop members-only site to house course
· Write sales letter and design landing pages

Brainstorm Blog Post Ideas

Your blog is like an animal whose appetite can't be satiated. It needs to be fed regularly and often. That means you must prepare a constant menu of blog post ideas.

Brainstorm blog post ideas below. Which ones can you cook up quickly to feed to your blog—and your hungry readers? Make sure the dish you prepare is beneficial to your readers!

Idea Spinning

Spark your creativity and productivity with idea spinning. If you have one book idea right now, consider spin-off ideas or titles you might develop in the future. For instance, if you want to write a book on container gardening, maybe you could write another on tomato container gardening, deck container gardening, and indoor container gardening. If you want to write a thriller, think of the series potential for the book and brainstorm about stories that feature secondary characters. You can spin one article idea into several pieces—or even a book—in the same way.

Below, spin your book, blog, article, and essay ideas into multiple ideas. Then choose the ones that get your mind spinning about the possibilities!

MY IDEA: _____

SPIN-OFF IDEAS:

1. _____

2. _____

3. _____

4. _____

5. _____

MY IDEA: _____

SPIN-OFF IDEAS:

1. _____

2. _____

3. _____

4. _____

5. _____

MY IDEA: _____

SPIN-OFF IDEAS:

1. _____

2. _____

3. _____

4. _____

5. _____

MY IDEA: _____

SPIN-OFF IDEAS:

1. _____

2. _____

3. _____

4. _____

5. _____

MY IDEA: _____

SPIN-OFF IDEAS:

1. _____

2. _____

3. _____

4. _____

5. _____

Enter Bloggers' Paradise

Your blog might feel like the bane of your existence and a drain on your creative resources. Every day or every week you have to come up with new posts. You see this as a necessary evil to build author platform and authority. Although blogging requires you to write, the endeavor doesn't feel creative.

But it can be—if you have a blog plan. By planning your blog content by month or week, you enter Bloggers' Paradise. When you plan to blog passionately about topics that inspire you and use your creative abilities to build your platform post by post, you

won't ever stare at the screen again and wonder what to blog about.

Create a one-month—or even a three-month—blog plan. (Use the information from the "Brainstorm Blog Post Ideas" exercise.) Choose a theme for each month, and write posts based on that theme. Or look at the themes and topics that run through your work. Create categories related to these topics, and then alternate them in your posts.

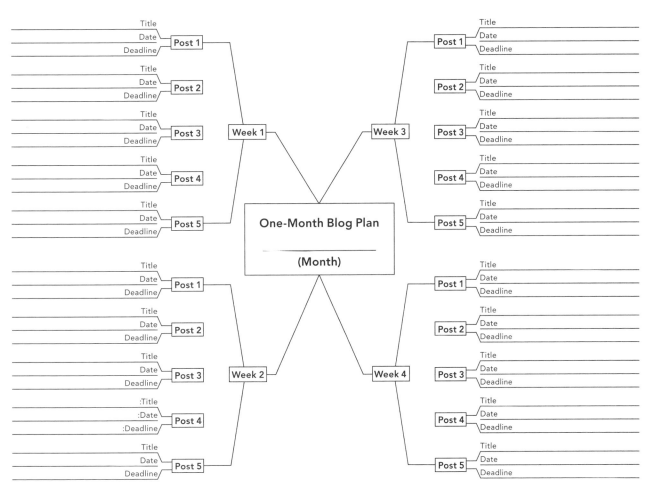

Design Your Website's Home Page

If you could have your dream author website, what would it look like? Draw it below. You may want to include the following:

- a headshot
- information on how to follow you on social media
- a tagline that states the benefit you offer site visitors or a statement about who you are (or how you want to be known) as an author
- a banner
- colors that mean something to you and appeal to and engage visitors

- a "lead magnet" (something you give away for free in return for an e-mail address)
- Individual pages (e.g., About, Products and Services, Media, Blog, Books, or any other pages you want)
- a way for readers to share your pages or posts

Log Your Ideas

You get new ideas all the time. Encourage your subconscious mind to continue sending them to the surface by acknowledging the ideas as they come, in the form of an idea log.

Log your ideas in the chart below.

Idea Log

Just because you think your idea is good doesn't mean it is. Your job is to evaluate every idea, whether it's for a book, an essay, an article, a blog post, or a product or service related to your writing, and determine if it's worthy of pursuit.

What's a good idea? One that serves and sells. That means it has to provide value and benefit for your readers, and it has to be unique and necessary in the marketplace.

Use the following chart to keep track of ideas worth pursuing. You also can use it to remind yourself of ideas that need improving!

Idea	Rating		
	□ Good	□ Bad	□ So-So
	□ Good	□ Bad	□ So-So
	□ Good	□ Bad	□ So-So
	□ Good	□ Bad	□ So-So
	□ Good	□ Bad	□ So-So
	□ Good	□ Bad	□ So-So

Keep Track of "Wet" Ideas

You step into the shower after a long day of ideating and creating. As the water pours over you and you wash your hair, suddenly an amazing idea pops into your mind.

That idea did not come out of your bottle of shampoo. Research shows that you're more likely to have a creative epiphany when performing a monotonous task, like showering. As you do something mindless, your brain switches to autopilot, which allows your subconscious to work on other things. It plays a game of free association.

As with daydreaming, mindless or monotonous activities relax the prefrontal cortex, which is the brain's center for decisions, goals, and behavior. They also clear the pathways that connect different regions of your brain. When your cortex is loose and your pathways are clear, new and creative ideas pop up more frequently.

Your brain behaves differently under a deadline. If you try to force yourself to come up with a good idea, your prefrontal cortex tightens up and increases

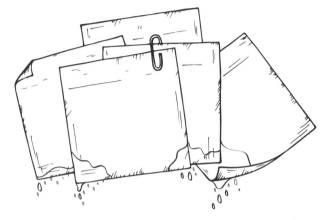

control. This improves your focus and gives you the ability to manage your attention, which works great for some people and in some situations. But it can cause you to feel less creative, too. When you focus on a task, your brain actually censors unconventional—creative—ideas or solutions.

Back to the shower. Given that you are likely to have great "wet" ideas, you want to keep track of them.

Use this page to write them down *immediately* after you get out of the tub. Or, better yet, purchase a product like Aqua Notes, a waterproof notepad you can hang in your shower!

_____

_____

_____

_____

_____

_____

_____

_____

Remember Your Night-Light Ideas

When you lie down in bed at night, your brain rests for a few moments before you fall asleep. With nothing else to distract it, your subconscious ideas and thoughts bubble up to the surface.

However, if the light bulb goes on just before you fall asleep, one of two things typically happens:

1. You fall asleep and don't remember the idea in the morning, which is really annoying.
2. The idea keeps you awake for hours.

Solve this problem by putting an idea journal next to your bed. Or use this page to jot down your night-light ideas. As with dreams, sometimes writing down your ideas before you go back to sleep can help you remember them more easily in the morning. When you wake up, make sense of what you wrote.

Date	Night-Light Idea

Use Competition Creatively

Exploring competing or complementary works sparks ideas and creativity. When you see what other writers or authors have done well—or not so well—you get ideas about how to improve your project, provide more benefit to your readers, and produce something unique and necessary in a category or market.

To do this, examine five to ten articles, essays, blogs, or books similar to your current idea. Then answer these questions:

What do you like about them? Why?

_____

_____

_____

What did the writer or author do well?

_____

_____

_____

What do you not like about them? Why?

_____

_____

_____

What could the writer or author have done better?

_____

_____

_____

How could you use what you discovered to improve your idea or project?

_____

_____

_____

Start a Side Project

Feeling uncreative? Turn your attention to something else.

You may feel you hardly have time for your writing project—and everything that goes with it—but research proves that side projects make you more creative and productive. Both the driving service Uber and the Google e-mail service Gmail started as side projects and grew into million-dollar and million-user enterprises. Also, in 2004, Google implemented a 20 percent rule for its employees, allowing them to spend up to 20 percent of their time exploring fun, passionate side projects. As a result, the other 80 percent of the employees' time became more productive and creative.

San Francisco State University psychology professor Dr. Kevin Eschleman and his colleagues measured the effect of creative hobbies on work. They discovered that employees with a creative hobby were more likely to be helpful, collaborative, and *creative*.

You need downtime from your work, but watching television or engaging in other escapist activities won't improve your creativity. You boost your creativity more significantly if you seek meaningful leisure activities that support your personal growth and development.

That's where side projects and hobbies come in. They provide a creative and fulfilling version of downtime that rejuvenates your writing.

Do you have a side project or creative hobby? If not, find one! It does not need to relate to your work, nor does it need to earn money. You might garden, take photographs, or build birdhouses, for example.

Draw your side project or hobby below, and commit to pursuing it on a regular basis.

Focus on Serving Others

You may have heard the advice "Write for your readers, not for yourself." This doesn't just help sell your work but also aids you in producing the most creative work. If you focus your writing project on how it serves others, you'll increase your creative capacity.

Research has proven that if you think your work will be used by someone else, you develop more unique ideas. On the other hand, if you believe you are the only one who will use the end product, you have fewer unique ideas.

As you think about your writing project, consider how others will use, enjoy, and incorporate what you've written into their lives. Answer the questions below.

Who will use your written work? Why?

_____

_____

_____

_____

How can you create for your readers?

_____

_____

_____

_____

How will your readers use your work?

_____

_____

_____

_____

_____

How will your creation affect or transform the lives of your readers?

_____

_____

_____

_____

_____

Draw a picture of how someone might use or be affected by your written words.

Deadlines Are Your Friends

Some people find they are most creative under pressure. Others feel stuck when they encounter a deadline. (To understand why, reread "Keep Track of 'Wet' Ideas.")

If you find deadlines helpful, try imposed mini-deadlines to get your creative juices flowing fast and often! They can help you tap into your creativity quickly and effectively.

Try writing for twenty-five minutes at a time and then taking a five- or ten-minute break, as the Pomodoro Technique suggests. (See pomodorotech nique.com for more.) Then start again. (Make sure to remove any outside distractions during this time.) Or write for fifty minutes, and then take a break.

You can decide to finish your article or essay by the end of the week. Determine how many words you need to write each day. Use that as a deadline; you must complete that word count by day's end each day of the week (until finished).

The short daily bursts of writing (with breaks to re-energize and clear your mind) work best when you are trying to increase both creativity and productivity.

Set a timer for your chosen amount of time. Then write. Keep track of two things: how creative you feel and how productive you are. Then compare this to times when you write without an imposed mini-deadline.

Writing Session Date	How creative do you feel?	How productive do you feel?

Take the Path of Most Resistance

The path of least resistance is enticing. I understand. We want easy.

However, if you want to become more creative, switch your attitude and jump on the path of *most* resistance.

Research shows that most of us naturally build on older or existing concepts when we create something new or brainstorm. This can lead to fewer creative ideas. You will design more creative ideas when you place restrictions on yourself while creating. Send your brain into overdrive, and prevent yourself from relying on past successes as the foundation of your current projects.

Try limiting the nature of a writing task. Dr. Seuss wrote *Green Eggs and Ham* after betting he couldn't produce a story using fewer than fifty words. Develop some restrictions on your writing. For example, if you normally write 1,500-word short stories, write one in fewer than 750 words. If your essays are always based on your own experiences, branch out by exploring someone else's. If you've only written 1,000-word magazine articles, produce some 250- to 300-word short pieces. If you normally write your books "off the top of your head," employ interviews with or anecdotes from other people. Or push yourself to use more creative words, specific words, or a certain type of sentence structure.

Writing Project	Self-Imposed Restriction

Write to Music

Certain types of music boost creativity and focus by stimulating the part of the brain that controls motor skills, emotions, and creativity. If you want to turn up your creativity, turn up the music while you work.

Jamming to your favorite upbeat songs may give your creativity a jolt. However, you might need something more soothing. Try out different songs and styles, and note which ones inspire you most. Also bear in mind the "Mozart Effect." Studies have shown that listening to Mozart's music increases creativity, clarity, concentration, and other cognitive functions.

Music from the baroque tradition stimulates creativity as well. It stabilizes mental, physical, and emotional rhythms so you can concentrate more deeply. Consider listening to Bach, Handel, Telemann, or any music at a pace of fifty to eighty beats per minute. You can use an app like Focus at Will, which provides music that will help you home in on your work.

Turn on some music. See how it affects your creativity and ability to write. Create a creativity playlist below.

Album or Song	Composer or Artist

Meditate Your Way to Creativity

If your mind is whirling and you feel confused, stressed, and overwhelmed, or you can't generate even one idea, stop. Remove your hands from the keyboard. Take a few deep breaths, and clear your mind. Don't think. Just sit. Be.

That's right—I'm asking you to meditate.

Studies have shown that meditation helps you tap into both convergent and divergent thinking modes, which affect your creative ability. Divergent thinking allows for the generation of many new ideas in a situation where more than one solution is correct. Convergent thinking, on the other hand, emphasizes speed, accuracy, and logic to generate one possible solution to a particular problem.

Meditation helps you generate new ideas and improves your mood, which also boosts creativity. A positive approach helps when you need to free yourself from a "stuck" place.

You can meditate for two minutes, twenty minutes, or longer. Try one of the many meditation techniques available. Focus on your breathing (in and out, in and out), try Brendon Burchard's Release Meditation Technique (repeat the word *release* as you breathe in and out), or learn Transcendental Meditation or mindfulness meditation. Any type of meditation will quiet your mind and help you write or generate ideas.

You also can use the coloring pages in the Focus section to meditate.

Keep a notebook handy so you can jot down your ideas as they pop into your head. (Trying to remember them after a meditation session can be difficult and distract you while you meditate.) Then go back to meditating.

Meditate now. Start with a simple period in which you focus on your breathing. Write about your experience below. Or draw whatever images popped into your head while you meditated.

Use a Pen and Paper

If you aren't feeling as creative as you'd like, turn off your computer and pick up a pad of paper and a pen. Write a book chapter, essay, article, or blog post by hand.

Carrie Barron, MD, and Alton Barron, MD, authors of *The Creativity Cure*, suggest that writing by hand enhances creativity. Maybe the key lies in the experience of writing by hand—the feel of the pen in your hand, the smell of the ink or the new notebook. Whatever the secret, you'll find that doing so helps you get into a creative flow.

Use this space to write a new blog post, essay, article, or book chapter.

Take a Daydream Break

If deadlines, restrictions, meditation, and the other suggestions in this section don't work for you, take a break to daydream. (Deliberately daydream!) Notice what happens when you just let your mind wander wherever it likes and leave it to its own devices.

When you allow your mind to wander, you generate more creative approaches to problem solving. Re-mind yourself of the problem you need to solve or the idea you need to create, and write it below. Then zone out for five or ten minutes. Just let your thoughts go where they will. Write down the solutions or ideas that come to you during that time.

THE PROBLEM I NEED TO SOLVE OR THE PROJECT FOR WHICH I NEED TO GENERATE AN IDEA: _____

_____

SOLUTIONS OR IDEAS: _____

_____

_____

_____

_____

Get out of the Box

You don't need to be in your office to work. In fact, working outside your office could improve your creativity.

Try sitting outside your office—yes, outside—venturing into nature, or going to a coffee shop, the library, or any location other than your office. An interesting study, conducted by Angela Leung of Singapore Management University and her co-authors from the University of Michigan and Cornell University, among others, proved that people who literally sat outside a box created outside-the-box ideas. They thought more creatively than those who sat in the box.

You may not sit in a cubicle, which is boxlike, or in a cardboard box, but you can move out of the room in which you work and instead sit in the hallway!

Try it. See what happens. Journal below about your experience.

_____

_____

_____

_____

_____

_____

                                                     _____

                                                     _____

Change Your Position

You spend your days *sitting* in front of a computer. To enhance your creativity, try lying down instead.

Researchers have discovered that people solve problems, like anagrams, more easily when they lie down rather than sit up. So take your laptop to the couch with you!

Also try standing up. A standing desk is good for your health, but you might find the position spurs new ideas, creative energy, or productivity, too.

Think Positively

Your attitude, which includes your thoughts and beliefs, affects your creativity. If you feel depressed, get out of bed on the wrong side of it, or continually tell yourself that you don't have any ideas or that you suffer from writer's block, you will find it hard to develop new concepts or churn out manuscript pages.

The *Harvard Business Review* reported that people who work with a positive mind-set experience increased productivity, engagement with their work, and creativity. They also work better in the face of challenges like deadlines.

Don't wait until you become successful to feel happy and positive! Cultivate that mind-set now to help you succeed.

- Write down three things for which you feel grateful. (Better yet, keep a daily gratitude journal.)
- Write or say an affirmation for two minutes. (See the Focus section of this book.)
- Color one of the pages in the Focus section of this book.
- Meditate for ten minutes.
- Describe your latest achievement (large or small).
- Exercise.
- Pay attention to your thoughts and spoken words by turning negative statements into positive ones, such as "I'm not an author … yet!" or "My queries have always been rejected … until recently.")

Close Your Eyes

Visual images and information bombard you daily. This overload doesn't help your creative ability. To avoid burnout, black it all out briefly.

Shut your eyes for one to five minutes. Allow your eyes and your mind to rest from the constant light and movement.

Then move your eyes back and forth while closed. Gently slide them to the left and then to the right. Doing so facilitates interaction between the right and left hemispheres of the brain, which boosts creativity.

What did you see with your eyes closed? Draw it (or write about it) below.

Write When You Feel Tired

Typically, you are more productive when rested and fully awake, but studies show that being tired helps your creativity. (No more excuses about not writing because you are too tired!)

Time of day has little effect on your ability to solve analytical problems. You will have more success when you feel less awake.

If you are a morning person, morning might seem the optimal time to solve a problem. But sometimes you are too focused when you are wide awake; this makes you screen out anything that doesn't seem relevant. Morning people's inhibitions are lower in the evening, which allows stray thoughts to enter their mind. These random thoughts combine with primary thoughts about a problem and generate a creative solution.

Try scheduling your creative tasks during the time of day when you feel least awake or more sluggish, such as during an afternoon slow-down, first thing in the morning, or just before bed.

If you are a morning person, try writing at night. If you are a night owl, try writing first thing in the morning. Or generate that idea you need for your next writing project before you take a nap in the afternoon.

When is your optimal writing time? When are you most awake and alert?

_____

At what time of day do you feel sleepy and sluggish?

_____

Try writing at a different time of day. Are you more creative? Keep track of what happens in the chart below.

Writing Time	Productivity	Creativity
	☐ More Productive ☐ Less Productive	☐ More Creative ☐ Less Creative
	☐ More Productive ☐ Less Productive	☐ More Creative ☐ Less Creative
	☐ More Productive ☐ Less Productive	☐ More Creative ☐ Less Creative
	☐ More Productive ☐ Less Productive	☐ More Creative ☐ Less Creative
	☐ More Productive ☐ Less Productive	☐ More Creative ☐ Less Creative

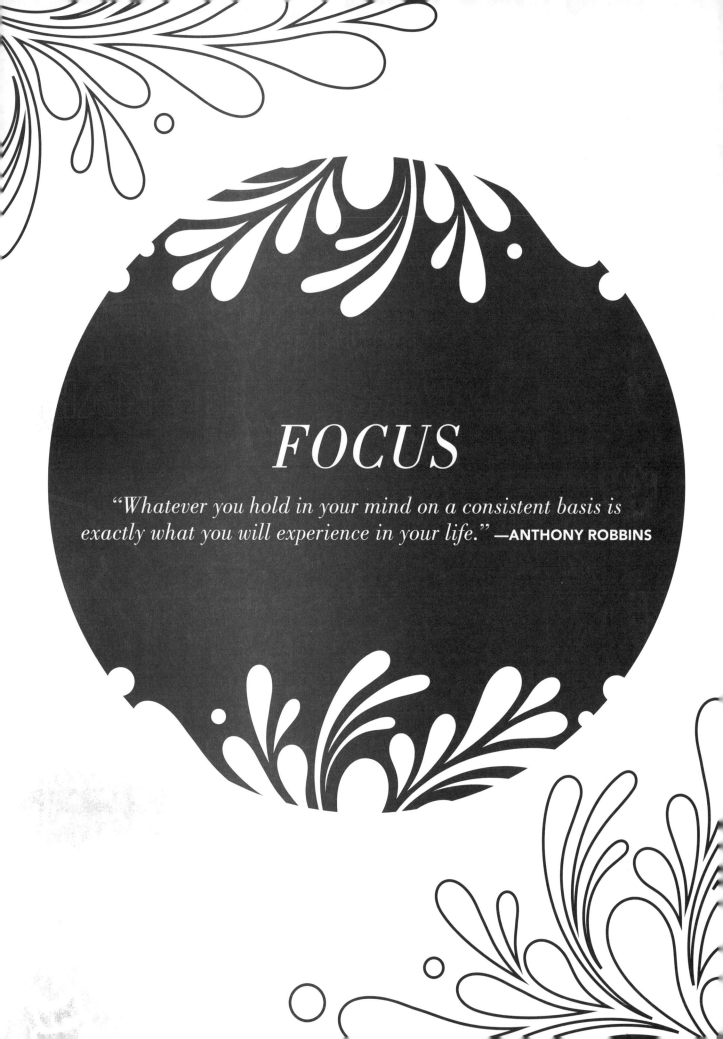

FOCUS

"Whatever you hold in your mind on a consistent basis is exactly what you will experience in your life." —ANTHONY ROBBINS

Can You Manage Your Attention?

You have an idea for an article, an essay, a blog, or a book. You want to become a professional writer, a published author, or a blogger. You'd like to become more creative or productive. Help yourself accomplish these goals, bring your ideas into the world, and develop your writing career by focusing on what you want to create.

To do so, take advantage of the benefits in this section: the meditative power of coloring and colors, and the motivational boost you receive from affirmations. Allow your mind to focus. Gain clarity. Relax. Give your ideas a chance to gestate and grow so you can coax them into the world easily and effectively.

Manage your attention. Dwell on thoughts that serve you, and visualize where you want to go. Think and feel more positive and able to reach your dream.

Each one of the following pages offers you an opportunity to spend time coloring or writing an affirmation. The coloring pages depict various dreams: a completed manuscript, your published novel in a bookstore, a literary agency contract, and more. As you color each page, imagine yourself experiencing whatever it illustrates, such as the sensation of holding your published book in your hands. What would that be like? To get the most benefit from these pages, visualize and feel as you color.

Additionally, the affirmation pages provide the chance to focus on a positive thought. It's most effective to write each affirmation at least twenty times. You can alternate the affirmation verbiage in this way:

- I am now a successful author.
- I, [name], am now a successful author.

If these positive statements don't feel true to you, alter them to fit this structure:

- Every day I get closer to my goal of becoming a successful author.
- Every day, I, [name], get closer to my goal of becoming a successful author.

Once you feel more confident in your affirmation, you can progress to the more definitive structure.

COLORING PAGES

"Your attitude is like a box of crayons that color your world. Constantly color your picture gray, and your picture will always be bleak. Try adding some bright colors to the picture by including humor, and your picture begins to lighten up."—**ALLEN KLEIN**

Writing

Book on Sale

Writing Retreat

Royalty Check

Royalty Payment Co.

1,000 — °°/100

$1000

Literary Agency Contract

Publishing Agency Contract

Public Speaker

Raving Fans

AFFIRMATION PAGES

"It's the repetition of affirmations that leads to belief. And once that belief becomes a deep conviction, things begin to happen."—**MUHAMMAD ALI**

I am a successful author.

_____
_____
_____
_____
_____
_____
_____
_____
_____
_____
_____
_____
_____
_____
_____
_____
_____
_____
_____
_____
_____

I combine my passion and purpose and feel inspired to take action every day!

I know I can

_____!

I promote my work willingly and well.

I'm committed to promoting my work!

I take little steps toward my goal.

People love to read what I write.

My words transform lives.

I have an Author Attitude.

I take action to help fulfill my potential.

_____

_____

_____

_____

_____

_____

_____

_____

_____

_____

_____

_____

_____

_____

_____

_____

_____

_____

_____

_____

_____

I see possibility and
potential even in
my challenges.

_____

_____

_____

_____

_____

_____

_____

_____

_____

_____

_____

_____

_____

_____

_____

I am a positive, joyous, and passionate person.

I know I am good enough,
have enough, and am
enough to succeed.

I overflow with creativity!

I always have an abundance of ideas.

I can write anytime and anywhere.

My words flow easily and effortlessly onto the page.

I can write a book that readers want, need, and buy!

_____

_____

_____

_____

_____

_____

_____

_____

_____

_____

_____

_____

_____

_____

_____

_____

I can produce a bestseller!

I have a consistent and effective writing practice or habit.

_____

_____

_____

_____

_____

_____

_____

_____

_____

_____

_____

_____

_____

_____

_____

_____

People are willing to pay me for my knowledge, stories, and creativity.

I have a lucrative and fulfilling career as a writer.

_____
_____
_____
_____
_____
_____
_____
_____
_____
_____
_____
_____
_____
_____
_____
_____
_____
_____
_____
_____
_____
_____

I am open to receive.

_____

_____

_____

_____

_____

_____

_____

_____

_____

_____

_____

_____

_____

_____

_____

_____

_____

_____

_____

_____

_____

_____

_____

_____

Index